LABELS

LABELS

Destroying the lies God never gave you
and embracing the truths that He has

DEREK GRIFFON

CONTENTS

INTRODUCTION

Labels. What comes to your mind when you hear that word?

We love them and we hate them. Labels allow us to identify things and place them in a specific box. Labels can make us stay away or draw near. Labels give us the info that puts us in the know. Labels help us recognize, categorize, and even scrutinize.

For instance, when you buy milk, you look at the label that says when the milk expires. (These days, it seems like some milk expires two weeks before the expiration date! Smells like cottage cheese and queso dip!)

Before we decide what clothing or shoes to buy, we look at the label or the tag that tells us the size. It's after we try them on that determines if we want that style.

There are moments when we are so thankful and grateful for labels.

But what about when it comes to Humans?

Labels, as I said earlier, warrant people to either draw near or walk away.

Labels can also provide insight into how we respond to someone.

Labels from our own perspective can even limit us.

A peer of yours, who was quoted in the book *The Three Big Questions That Change Every Teenager,* said, *"But people tend to **put you in a box** and only think of you a certain way once they get a **certain label** about you."* [1]

Do any of you have a certain label that has been placed on you?

Maybe it's Your **Reputation**: Someone spreads a rumor about you, and it's not fair for them to judge you based on it because you know that rumor is **a lie.**

Your **Personality**: Someone thinks you are overwhelming because you are too outgoing (extroverted) or too quiet and selfish because you are not the life of the party (introverted).

Your **Past**: Peers know something about you that you are guilty and ashamed of, and it immediately shuts them down from getting to know you. Or maybe you are holding on to something from your past that no one knows about, and you have labeled yourself by what you have done or what has happened to you.

Your **Goodness**: People think you are the good guy or girl. You do nothing wrong. You don't cuss or talk bad about others. When anyone mentions something inappropriate, your eyes get big because maybe you have never heard someone say "that" before. I have been there. When you are the "good kid" people feel like they can't be real around you because they want to respect your boundaries.

It hurts, doesn't it? You can have a "good" label and still people don't draw near, they stay back.

Again. Labels. We love them and hate them.
Do you know why?
Because it is someone's generalization of who we are.

If we're honest, we hate being labeled especially when that label...is **a lie.**
We hate being labeled because it can **limit** how others interact with us.
On the other hand, we love labels because it gives us the ability to decide how we treat others.

What if there was another way we can love and be secure?
I believe that we rely too much on status in this world, and it takes away the dignity of human beings,

causes distaste for image bearers, and creates misery in the human soul.

God created all things and saw that it was good. Most of all, this means his precious creation including you and me! [2]

When I was younger, I always hated being misunderstood. When I heard rumors about myself or when I heard about people not liking me, it drove me into hardcore insecurity. This insecurity was something I carried all throughout high school, even into college.

But in the last five to six years of my life, I'm honestly over it. I am by no means the most secure person on this planet, but I do know I am way more confident in who God has called me to be than I have ever been. He's called me to be Derek Griffon. He saved me from my sin through the cross of Christ and made me new through His Resurrection. I am a Pastor, but I am not your stereotypical suit-wearing-professional pastor. Sorry, if I wore that, it would be inauthentic. There's nothing wrong with it, but it's not me and there's no biblical argument for it.

I am tired of inauthenticity in this world. I am not the most sophisticated person you will ever meet. I tell it like it is, in a loving way. I am loud when I preach the word. I have twitches that I am aware of, and people point them out from time to time.

But when we change who we are or adapt to the labels we are given we are just trying to please everybody. I don't remember who said this, but you cannot please 100% of people 100% of the time.

That sounds like another label we need to get rid of: *People Pleaser!*

So, this one truth has hit me that I hope to drive into your brain throughout this book. This one bottom line is so freeing, even if it is the only thing you take away:

Don't ever take on a label that God never gave you!

When it comes down to it, it only matters what God says about you. It only matters the truths that Jesus speaks over you. The only status that really matters is that you are a child of God!

So, it's time to destroy the lies God never gave you and start embracing the truths that he has.

PART 1

FROM DAMAGED TO DELIVERED

CHAPTER 1
DAUGHTER

"God's love isn't based on me. It's simply placed on me. And it's the place from which I should live . . . loved."
Lysa TerKeurst

I have been in student ministry since I was 19 years old and have been able to hang out with teenagers from all different backgrounds. One common theme that keeps occurring is: We are all broken.

Every one of us has been damaged by something or someone in our lives. I hear countless stories of parents divorcing, addiction, affairs, alcohol abuse, sexual abuse, suicides, and so much more.

It doesn't take a genius or even a follower of Jesus to realize we live in a fractured world. Sadly, this brokenness is used to label us and others.

At the beginning of 2021, I was speaking at a Disciple Now retreat and I was talking to an adult leader when a student walked up. I talked with both of them for a few minutes and once the student walked away, this leader preceded to tell me that the student's dad had recently committed suicide. Not only that, but she was now the talk of the school and had the label of "That's the girl whose dad blew his head off."

The tragedy is horrible enough. But to be labeled by that damage in her life. To be reminded by rumors spread by others this is what she is known as? It broke my heart.

Because we are **not** our damages.
I want to remind you that Jesus was damaged on the cross so that you could be delivered from ever being labeled a damaged person.

Maybe you are like me. In a family that was split from divorce. My parents divorced when I was too young to understand exactly what happened. As I got older, I started to wonder, "will that be my story one day?"

You see, we can allow the damages of our past and even our present to define us. But the beauty of the gospel is that God no longer sees you as damaged, He sees you as delivered.

I want to explore together the story of a woman who was damaged for 12 years, but after an encounter with Jesus, her life was changed forever.

This story occurs in Matthew 5:21-34:

21 When Jesus had crossed over again by boat to the other side, a large crowd gathered around him while he was by the sea. 22 One of the synagogue leaders, named Jairus, came, and when he saw Jesus, he fell at his feet 23 and begged him earnestly, "My little daughter is dying. Come and lay your hands on her so that she can get well and live." 24 So Jesus went with him, and a large crowd was following and pressing against him.

Jesus was always looking to make a difference in people's lives. He came to this earth with what Dr. Tony Evans refers to as "the kingdom agenda". [1] The kingdom agenda is to restore humanity to peace and order through his sacrifice on the cross and resurrection. Jesus' mission has never ceased!

Now check this out, as Jesus was headed to make a change in the life of a young girl who was dying, another encounter happens. Jesus demonstrates in this story the "As you go" command that he gives us in the great commission.

25 Now a woman suffering from bleeding for twelve years 26 had endured much under many doctors. She had spent everything she had and was not helped at all. On the contrary, she became worse. 27 Having heard about Jesus, she came up behind him in the crowd and touched his clothing. -- Matthew 5:25-27. (CSB)

This woman was suffering from bleeding for 12 years. Imagine facing a disease or something medical that no one can solve. Imagine the pain and the discomfort. Because of this woman's condition, she was deemed untouchable, unclean, destitute. She was **damaged**. She probably felt worthless. She was basically bleeding to death. And because she had a reputation for 12 years that she was indeed untouchable, and unclean she was labeled with this burden: Damaged goods. Bleeder. Hopeless.

I think there are four dynamics we see in this woman that we can relate to:

*Number one: **She's burdened***

We live in a burdensome world. And some of you have a burden like this woman did. You are suffering from SOMETHING.

People make your burden worse by defining you by it:

Your parents divorced. "That's the boy whose parents no longer love each other."
You have a debilitating disease. "That's the girl with _____."
You cut yourself and it shows. "That's the cutter."
Maybe you are dying. For years in a student ministry, I led a girl in our youth group who was dying with a broken liver, and you could see it from the color in her

face. It was hard to hear her name and not think "that's the girl who is dying."

A rumor has been eating you alive. And you know the rumor is not true!

You have anxiety constantly, so you label yourself. "I am a worrier..."

You are depressed. You don't leave your room or your house. So now you are referred to as agoraphobic.

As I am sitting here writing this, I am watching College GameDay, and I hear that the Coach of Ohio State football, Ryan Day's dad committed suicide when he was 31. And he was made fun of for not having a dad! How evil and horrifying is this? He was labeled... "You have no dad!" Over time he would not want to mention his dad's suicide to avoid being labeled as fatherless.

Whatever it is, you have a burden.
It's deep and it's eating you alive.

Number two: **She's broken**

25 Now a woman suffering from bleeding for twelve years26 had endured much under many doctors. She had spent everything she had and was not helped at all. On the contrary, she became worse. -- Mark 5:26 (CSB)

She became broke because of her investment in trying to get well. Doctors could do nothing for her, for 12 years! What's crazy is the very girl that Jesus was headed to heal before this encounter was 12 years old. The very disease that has been crippling this woman for years is the same amount of years as this dying pre-teen has been alive. And they are both dying.

Place yourself in this woman's shoes for a moment. What if you were told "There is nothing we can do. You are essentially bleeding to death. You are currently on your deathbed." That is a label no one wants to hear.

You might be similar in that you're broken because you are finding and investing in things to take your own pain away. But nothing is working.
Maybe it is drugs or relationship after relationship. And your burdens and brokenness become worse.

However, this brokenness can lead to something that works for you in the same way it worked for this woman. This leads to the next point.

*Number three: **She's desperate***

27 Having heard about Jesus, she came up behind him in the crowd and touched his clothing. 28 For she said, "If I just touch his clothes, I'll be made well." 29 Instantly her flow of blood ceased, and she sensed in her body that she was healed of her affliction. -- Mark 5:27-29 (CSB)

Have you ever felt SO Desperate that you are at your wits' end? Have you ever been so desperate that nothing, not crowds or fear could keep you away from faith because faith is all that you have left?

This woman, considered unclean and damaged, probably had heard about this man named Jesus. This man is the talk of the town because of His healing power. She wanted to touch this miracle worker.

Understand again that most who knew this woman would have been frightened or looked down on her because she was unclean. But again...*she was desperate.*

Charles Martin, author of various books sums it up well:

> "Being unclean, she cannot get to where He is. They won't let her. The law prohibits it. She knows she is not allowed around other people. She's been forced to live and sustain herself on the outskirts, and - if she knows anything at all - she is certainly not allowed to reach out and touch anyone. Most of all, Him. But she doesn't care what they think. She has come to the end of herself." [2]

I want you to feel this: ***Desperation will lead us to do bold things and take brave chances.***

I can imagine her making her way through the crowd, tired, weary, in tears and trying to get to Jesus. Crowds swarming. And she makes this last chance attempt at just touching the cloak of Jesus. Jesus, the only clean one to ever live in this world, cleaned this unclean woman of her discharge. She was healed instantly!

But I want you to see the best healing she got as we finish out the story:

30 Immediately Jesus realized that power had gone out from him. He turned around in the crowd and said, "Who touched my clothes?"

31 His disciples said to him, "You see the crowd pressing against you, and yet you say, 'Who touched me?'"

32 But he was looking around to see who had done this. 33 The woman, with fear and trembling, knowing what had happened to her, came and fell down before him, and told him the whole truth. 34 "<u>Daughter</u>," he said to her, "<u>your faith has saved you</u>. Go in peace and be healed from your affliction." -- Mark 5:30-34 (CSB)

As you see this leads us to the fourth and greatest dynamic of this woman: **SHE WAS DELIVERED!**

Did you grasp what just happened? This woman went from being labeled as damaged, to being labeled as DAUGHTER! The words of the most powerful, most loving man to ever walk this earth called her DAUGHTER!

The teachings of Jesus reveal a profound truth that human beings, through faith in Jesus, can become family members of the one true God. Salvation was described in birthing or legal terms, indicating a family relationship. What an incredible metaphor for the Christian experience! When we are born into this world, because of the brokenness of humanity, we are already damaged and lost orphans. Yet because of Jesus' death on the cross, we can be called sons and daughters of the one true God, our Father!

Feel this: **When you reach out to Jesus in desperation, you will be delivered.**

For those of you ladies who feel damaged because of what you've been through: **You are not damaged, you are a DAUGHTER.**

For those of you guys out there who feel like your scum, I want you to know you are not scum, **you are a Son!**

11

For this woman, Jesus was her last and final hope.
No matter what you are going through and no
matter how you have been labeled, just like this
woman:
***Jesus is your last and only hope to be fully
delivered.***

All you have to do...**is reach out**. This is what this
woman did.
No problem is too big for Him to handle.
You are one prayer away from your label being ripped
off by Jesus and replaced with the truth.

**When desperate people run to Jesus, they are
spiritually delivered.**

As a student pastor, I have the honor and privilege of
coaching some phenomenal small group leaders. I
once had a small group leader reach out about a
student who went into her group for the first time
after one of our Student Sunday Night worship
services.

My leader proceeded to tell me that this student
assumed there was some type of mistake and that
she was in this small group because she identified as
a boy.

Pause: Immediately when most people hear this, it's
not just a red flag, it's a warning. A lot of churches
might hear this and freak out because our labels say

that "certain people" **do not belong** in the church. But on a night where we talked about keeping it real in small groups, it definitely got real!

What I love about our church and especially this small group leader is that though doctrinally and theologically we believe that God made a man to be a man and a woman to be a woman, we decided we're going to love this girl like crazy regardless of what she believed.

Instead of being like a bunch of bigots and trying to argue what's right and what's wrong, *we chose to dignify a person made in God's image*. Because here's the truth: **We don't have to agree with people to accept them!**

My small group leader and I had many conversations about this very thing: *How to love a person, not label them, and love them with truth and grace.* She started having many conversations with this girl and even though this particular student didn't agree with the leader on many of the things she said, she kept coming back. She kept going to her small group. She even went to camp with us over the summer and we started seeing a huge difference in her. Not because we had this agenda to change who she was identifying as, but to love her and get her to Jesus! And in the midst of loving her well, Jesus would begin transforming her.

Through many conversations with this student, our leader learned more about her earthly father's issues. And whenever there is a dad issue in the home, wreckage is not far. And this is what she experienced. As we empathized with her, we saw that she was not confident that she could call herself a daughter of her father. Frustration because of the turmoil in her life is the thing that potentially played a part in her choosing another identity. These are the kinds of things students reveal that will break your heart!

We started the series Labels based on this book, and that first night I talked about this very story of the woman with the discharge and how she was no longer damaged, but that now she heard the words of the Savior of the world that changed her forever - "**Daughter**." As I talked about the reality that when Jesus saves us, he also makes us new, and he also ushers us into the family of God so we can be called sons and daughters, I looked to my left as I spoke and saw this student.

She was in tears. I could sense God speaking to her at that moment. That night, I gave an invitation to the students for anyone to receive Jesus as Lord and Savior. Normally I would have them stand or raise their hand but on this particular night I didn't because we had a different kind of ending to the night. And this is where it continued to be a move of God.

That night there were two label papers on each student's seat and three paper shredders at the front of the worship center. I told students to write down a label they wanted to destroy and shred it so they could put on a new label: The truth of what God says about them.

Right after service, I was collecting the connection cards of those who wanted to respond and receive Jesus. There were seven salvations that night, and right when I started reading the first card, I noticed the very name of the student we have been talking about in this story!

She checked the box that said she wanted to give her life to Jesus and I was in awe! But I'm not sure that was even the best part. I looked down at the bottom of the connection card and she had written something.

She wrote this:
"I want to finally be a **daughter**!"

How powerful is THAT!
This is it! This is why we don't label, but love! This is why Jesus didn't label, but loved!

Through the love of Jesus, the incredible love of our small group leader, and the desire to not give up on someone who was going through gender confusion, this student is now changed, made new, and is excited about being called "Daughter!" By the one true Jesus! If that doesn't make you leap with excitement in your heart I don't know what will!

She destroyed the label of "damaged" that night and embraced the truth of being a daughter! She was vulnerable and utterly real with the Savior of the world. She was desperate for a loving Father to love her unconditionally and she got the greatest Father ever in Father God! She recently took her next step in baptism!

I love what Brant Hansen says in his book The Truth About Us:

> "Desperation wins. It always does. It's a theme that rings through everything Jesus said and did. Those who are at the very end of themselves, desperate enough to humbly throw themselves vulnerably at the feet of God, with no excuses, will find exactly what they're yearning for." [3]

When desperate people reach out to Jesus, they are spiritually delivered.

Just in case you don't remember, at the beginning of this story in Mark 5, Jesus was headed somewhere else before he healed this woman. He was headed to heal the 12-year-old daughter of synagogue leader

Jairus. I can imagine Jairus being overwhelmed and frustrated that he asked for the healing of his daughter first! There was no time Jesus, come on! The rest of the story reads like this:

35 While he was still speaking, people came from the synagogue leader's house and said, "Your daughter is dead. Why bother the teacher anymore?"

36 When Jesus overheard what was said, he told the synagogue leader, "Don't be afraid. Only believe." 37 He did not let anyone accompany him except Peter, James, and John, James's brother. 38 They came to the leader's house, and he saw a commotion — people weeping and wailing loudly. 39 He went in and said to them, "Why are you making a commotion and weeping? The child is not dead but asleep." 40 They laughed at him, but he put them all outside. He took the child's father, mother, and those who were with him, and entered the place where the child was. 41 Then he took the child by the hand and said to her, "Talitha koum" (which is translated, "Little girl, I say to you, get up"). 42 Immediately the girl got up and began to walk. (She was twelve years old.) At this they were utterly astounded. 43 Then he gave them strict orders that no one should know about this and told them to give her something to eat. -- Mark 5:35-43 (CSB)

The people from the synagogue told Jairus to give up essentially. However, Jesus wasn't done with his healing tour. Jesus showed up and woke this little girl up! Jesus proved his ability once again to take someone from damaged to delivered! He brought this girl literally out of death into life! Jesus proved this to be true twice in a small time period! One woman is healed of her disease and is also saved by faith. The little girl was physically dead, but Jesus commanded her to be alive! Both of these ladies were healed physically, but most importantly they were healed spiritually!

No one remains damaged in the hands of the greatest restorer, Jesus!

Amen!

Reflect:

1. Where have you felt damaged or what have you been labeled in your life? Reflect on it.

2. Can you relate to the first three dynamics of this woman's life? Burdened? Broken? Desperate? How so?

3. Are you desperate enough to run to Jesus? How can he give you the peace and deliverance you need?

4. Write down a label that you need to destroy. Find a shredder. Shred the label that is a lie. Then, write down the truth God has given you and wear it as truth!

CHAPTER 2
NO LONGER CONDEMNED

"Guilt says "I made a mistake."
Shame says "I am a mistake."
Grace says "I'm Forgiven."
Lecrae

There is nothing more frustrating than a bully. A bully is someone who constantly uses words and actions to berate a person or persons. I've seen it all my life throughout school, on every social media outlet, and unfortunately in the Church. A bully likes to beat people down. A bully can be someone who is potentially so insecure in who they are that they must take that insecurity out on someone else to make themselves feel better or superior. A bully can be someone who is self-righteous and prideful. A person who knows the rules and places burdens on others by commenting on their lives and reminding others of their failures. They assume that guilt is the way to change someone to be more like them. I also realize that in a book on not labeling people I've chosen to label bullies...bullies. Fair. Let's just describe them as very mean people who dislike themselves enough to take it out on others. They need grace too.

Before the age of social media, students could leave school and not have to face a bully for another day. Now because our "friends" and followers are stuffed in our pockets, bullying can continue through the night. The more I have spoken to students and the more I hear of this issue the more my heart aches for the next generation.

For some reason bullies like putting people in their "place". They like to label and judge people based on what they see or perceive. It makes them feel good when they have made someone feel less than and worse than themselves. Sometimes they can be overly blunt about their opinion about others. They have this mentality that they can love someone without actually liking them. Maybe, if they're honest, they neither love nor like certain people. I am so glad Jesus doesn't just love me, but likes me as well.

Unfortunately, this bullying comes from a lot of Christians. Followers of Jesus who will allow their tongues to create fires. Just look at social media. Sometimes it's discrimination. Sometimes it's prejudice. Sometimes it's based on social status. Sometimes it's based on popularity. Sometimes it's republican vs democrat. Baptist vs Pentecostal. One Christian denomination that loves the one true God vs another Christian denomination that loves the one true God throwing one another under the bus. Go figure.

Maybe it's this attitude of "if you can't do for me, you're of no use to me, I want no part of you." Sometimes we want others to be ashamed or embarrassed.
Why is it that we would rather beat someone down rather than lift them up?

And for any of my older adult friends who think the next generation just needs to toughen up and get over it and stop being snowflakes, I want to remind you of something Jesus's half-brother James said:

"And the tongue is a fire. The tongue, a world of unrighteousness, is placed among our members. It stains the whole body, sets the course of life on fire, and is itself set on fire by hell." -- James 3:6 (CSB)

"Blessing and cursing come out of the same mouth. My brothers and sisters, these things should not be this way." -- James 3:10 (CSB)

Or how about this wise proverb:

"Death and life are in the power of the tongue, and those who love it will eat its fruit." -- Proverbs 18:21 (CSB)

Being mentally tough is so important. I agree. A guy like me who battles anxiety, I strive in the name of Jesus to be more mentally tough. But what happens when a person is constantly guilted and shamed into remembering horrible things that have happened in their lives? What happens when a person is constantly cut by the words of others and can't escape it because they follow them?

There was a story that came out a few years ago that struck me and angered me to my core. It was the story of a child who was the face of iconic Australian outback hat firm Akubra. At 14 years old, she took her own life over online bullying. The father invited the bullies to her funeral, saying: "If by some chance the people who thought this was a joke and made themselves feel superior by the constant bullying and harassment see this post, please come to our service and witness the complete devastation you have created." [1] As you can see, words have the power to take life.

How powerful is it that our tongues can create even more fragility in humans?
We cast ourselves as the judges and jurors when we really need to understand this: *We are HORRIBLE judges and jurors!* The gavel we hold is not one we have been gifted with. Our words can condemn others with guilt and shame, and it sends them to a

prison we have created. That is the label that bullies place on others: **Condemnation**.

It reminds me of the story of Jesus and his encounter with a woman who was caught in adultery. It is one of my favorite encounters that Jesus has with a broken beat-up person. A person who is in need of love and not judgment. A person who is guilty, shame-ridden, and embarrassed. What you are about to see in this story draws parallels to our time today, and how much power, judgment, and words can almost take a life.

If you have a Bible, shoot over to John 8:2-11:

2 At dawn he went to the temple again, and all the people were coming to him. He sat down and began to teach them.

3 Then the scribes and the Pharisees brought a woman caught in adultery, making her stand in the center. 4 "Teacher," they said to him, "this woman was caught in the act of committing adultery. 5 In the law Moses commanded us to stone such women. So what do you say?" -- John 8:2-5 (CSB)

Now before we continue in the story, I want you to imagine with me for a moment that someone caught you doing something horrible. I mean this thing is so bad that you knew if others knew about it, it could cost you your reputation or even your life. Or imagine someone found out about your past from a picture that was shared on social media.

Maybe you were sleeping with your significant other.
You were caught looking at porn.
You stole something from a friend or a store.
You were pocketing money from your parents and not being honest when they asked about it.
You cheated on the ACT or a big final at the end of the school year.
You took steroids or some type of supplement that enhanced your athleticism.

Now, what if whoever caught you kidnapped you, brought you to a Church, threw you in the middle of a crowd attending a bible study, and then played a video or posted the photo on a screen for everyone to see.

Imagine how you would feel in that moment. Your accusers are pointing at you while explaining the horrific thing you did. Everyone in that crowd starts to chime in and point their fingers at you because the evidence was immediately stacked against you.

You sit there as your shirt is drenched in tears. You are on the verge of a panic attack because you have been exposed to a bunch of your peers who now think you're scum. Guilt grips your lungs as you fight to breathe and shame severely pierces your soul. I am assuming you would wish you would die at that moment. I know I would.

You **feel** the judgment around you. You **see** the disappointing look in the eyes of people you know. You **sense** hatred. And there's no way out.

Now, go back and read over that text we just read.

In fact, let's read it in the Message Translation:

John 8 1-2 Jesus went across to Mount Olives, but he was soon back in the Temple again. Swarms of people came to him. He sat down and taught them.
3-6 The religion scholars and Pharisees led in a woman who had been caught in an act of adultery. They stood her in plain sight of everyone and said, "Teacher, this woman was caught red-handed in the act of adultery. Moses, in the Law, gives orders to stone such persons. What do you say?" They were trying to trap him into saying something incriminating so they could bring charges against him. (MSG)

Empathize with this woman for a moment. She is labeled "adulterer." Can you imagine being thrown in the middle of people you probably know, so that what you did could become your immediate label? Even if it is true that she committed the act, how do you think she felt? Damaged. She feels worthless, embarrassed, damaged, and worst of all...condemned or eternally damned.

And look at **why** they did it. They were trying to trap Jesus to get him arrested. Just to prove some point, just to trap Jesus in his words, they sought this woman, caught this woman, and dropped this woman in front of a crowd to see if Jesus had correct theology.

How sick is that? A woman is used and abused for self-righteous reasons and power. It's horrifying. This still happens today in our time.

So, empathize with her. Feel what she may have felt. Let it make you burn with rage!
That's what bullies do: They use what power they think they have to put someone in their place.

But what I love about Jesus, is that he brings hope to the hopeless, power to the powerless, peace to the broken, and love to those who are labeled!

And we are about to see this play out in this woman's life.

6 They asked this to trap him, in order that they might have evidence to accuse him.
Jesus stooped down and started writing on the ground with his finger. 7 When they persisted in questioning him, he stood up and said to them,

"The one without sin among you should be the first to throw a stone at her." 8 Then he stooped down again and continued writing on the ground. 9 When they heard this, they left one by one, starting with the older men. Only he was left, with the woman in the center. 10 When Jesus stood up, he said to her, "Woman, where are they? Has no one condemned you?"

11 "No one, Lord," she answered.

"Neither do I condemn you," said Jesus. "Go, and from now on do not sin anymore." -- John 8:6-11 (CSB)

There are three things I want you to see in this text that Jesus did that we can also do.

Number one: ***Jesus saw a soul, not scum. What does that mean for us? We are to see souls, not scum.***

The Pharisees saw a woman they believed deserved to die. There was no remorse for her. They saw her as scum. The super-religious chose to see someone as worthless. Someone who was worthy of death. Which according to the Law of Moses, she was.

But Jesus came to bring something new. According to Jesus, the ones who were clean on the outside but dirty on the inside deserved to die too. Everyone in that moment, except Jesus, was sinners. They were all worthy of death. But again, Jesus sees beyond our sin into our soul. **16 For God loved the world in this way: He gave his one and only Son, so that everyone who believes in him will not perish but have eternal life. -- John 3:16 (CSB).** This is the gospel: *God generously gave his son to seek, die for, and save souls!*

Once we have experienced this incredible grace, out of the abundance of our hearts, we shouldn't label others, we love others! We have a gospel worldview that sees all people as a soul!

I remember one time sitting in the cafe of our student ministry center in high school. I was at the table with a few of my best friends. We were having a great time chatting, eating, and chilling. We were about ten minutes from going up to our worship time in the big room when I saw two people about to walk in the front doors of the student ministry center. Now, I saw both of them walking up before my friends did. I already knew of their reputation. Isn't it pathetic how we let reputation alone define who someone is? Their reputation was as a couple who walked with the 'wrong crowd' and probably slept together.

I turned to my friends as they noticed the couple walking in and they asked the question, "What are *they* doing here?" Much snobbery was in this question. As if the two students walking in were about to corrupt the whole youth group. So instead of us being excited that two students could potentially meet Jesus that night, they worried about two sinners being in the mix of the Christians.

I remember boldly and deliberately getting furious, so I said, "You have got to be kidding me! So, these two show up and could possibly meet Jesus tonight. But because you know their sin and that they are sinners, you want them gone? Well, according to your theology, you should leave as well!" Jaws dropped.

Believe me, there were definitely moments where my self-righteous blood boiled when I knew what people did and wanted them to repent immediately. I didn't always want this in a loving way. It reminds me of what NF raps about in his song *10 Feet*: "Church is where I found God, but it's also where I learned to judge." [2] That's how I grew up. I feel like a lot of us can relate to what NF was saying. We find grace in the same place where we learn not to extend it. But at that moment, I felt for those two students. I felt the Lord speak to me to not see sinners as scum, but as souls who could be saved from their sin!

This leads me to point number two: ***Jesus stood up for the mistreated; therefore, we stand up for the mistreated***

How courageous is this: Jesus stood up and made a statement to the hypocrite: If you're not perfect, you have no right to condemn! Jesus essentially told the Pharisees what Andy Mineo says, "Before you hold a stone, hold a mirror." [3] When you live in the world of self-righteousness and wear that label like a badge of honor, you only see people for their sins and failures.

Brant Hansen makes a powerful statement: **"It's our self-righteousness that keeps us from really seeing people as they are."** [4]

Take off your worldly lens and put on the Word's lenses. Take off your lens of judgment and put on the lens of Jesus.

Have you ever almost gotten in a fight standing up for someone who is being treated like trash? Have you ever chosen to be a voice for the voiceless around you? It takes courage to help rip off a label of someone else so that you can show them how to embrace God's truth!

What if we did what Andy Stanley suggested instead: **"Be kind. Loan someone your strength instead of reminding them of their weaknesses."** [5]

This brings me to number three: *Jesus chose compassion over condemnation; therefore, we choose compassion over condemnation.*

This is so important for this generation. Use this as an anthem: It's time to **turn off condemnation** and **turn up compassion**!

This is what Jesus did!

Jesus also gave grace to the sinner. He turned up compassion in verse 11, *"No one has condemned you, neither do I. Go and sin no more."*

Jesus didn't condone her sin. He straight up told her not to sin anymore. But Jesus didn't condemn her either. Because he loved her.

For God so loved EVERYBODY! God so loved HER! Don't miss this next text that we don't often quote with John 3:16. It is in the next two verses:

17 For God did not send his Son into the world to condemn the world, but to save the world through him. 18 Anyone who believes in him is not condemned, but anyone who does not believe is already condemned, because he has not believed in the name of the one and only Son of God. -- John 3:17-18 (CSB)

NO condemnation.

Jesus would later be condemned on the cross for our sin so that our sin would be covered by His blood.

21 He made the one who did not know sin to be sin for us, so that in him we might become the righteousness of God. -- 2 Corinthians 5:21 (CSB)

Paul says in Romans, **Therefore, there is now no condemnation for those in Christ Jesus, -- Romans 8:1 (CSB)**

Jesus was the only perfect one who had the right to stone her, and he said: **"woman where are they? Has no one condemned you? She said, "No one Lord," And Jesus said "Neither do I condemn you; go, from now on sin no more"**

Jesus spoke life to this woman and though He had the right to stone her, he didn't take her life, he gave her life. **Jesus didn't lay the hammer down to condemn her, He would eventually lay His life down to save her!**

She must have felt what you might feel: Unlovable. Irredeemable. Damaged goods. But Jesus loves you and desires to redeem you. So, He became the damage and wreckage on the cross to prove to you that you are loved.

Though this story speaks of a mob seeking to destroy a woman, Jesus is showing us an example, to speak life into those around us.

Our words carry weight when used towards anyone. Our words can kill. Our words can give life.

Do you want to help people not be defined by the labels people give? I have a few tips:

- Find those who are *insecure* and give them *security*.
- Look out for those who *struggle* and give them *strength*.
- Pour into those who are *weak* and give them *power*.

If you can relate to the bully in this story, feel this: Bullying ain't cool, it's cowardly.
There is still time to repent and ask God to forgive you for your cowardice. You no longer have to wear the label of a punk. It's not who you are!

If you relate to the woman in this story, stop listening to the bullies that shame and guilt you!

Who is the last person the woman listened to and looked to in this story? The woman listened to Jesus!! She looked to Jesus!

I think Brene Brown hit the nail on the head when she said this in her book *The Gifts of Imperfection*,

"Shame works like the zoom lens on a camera. When we are feeling shame, the camera is zoomed in tight and all we see is our flawed selves, alone and struggling." [6]

She could have stayed zoomed in on her flaws and struggles but Jesus was there! And she chose to look up to and listen to Jesus! You need to do the same! Maybe others' words have made you contemplate taking your own life. I want you to feel this and believe this: No one has ever shown up to a funeral of a suicide and celebrated. You are too precious to allow any label to get in your head and convince you that life isn't worth living.

If you can relate to Jesus, turning up compassion and turning off condemnation, keep doing it! People are hurting! People are dying! We don't have time to judge someone for what they have been through! We don't have time to look at someone side-eyed. Because Jesus loves everyone, we too love everyone.

LISTEN TO JESUS! HIS VOICE LEADS YOU TO YOUR IDENTITY! HIS VOICE IS THE ONLY ONE THAT ULTIMATELY MATTERS!

I want to end this chapter with one more story. It is a story I heard on YouTube from Matt Chandler, Pastor of The Village Church. He was in college sitting in a class when he and a friend of his befriended a fellow classmate. Both of these guys were followers of Jesus, so their intent was to be a light in their classroom. They found out the girl they befriended was promiscuous, but they still decided to love her like Jesus. Matt had a friend who was playing a concert locally and he invited this girl to the concert knowing there would be a gospel presentation.

They arrived at the concert and were having a good time when the minister stepped up to the platform. He began his talk by saying "Today we're going to talk about sex" and according to Matt, this was an uh oh moment considering who they had brought with them. How would this minister handle this topic? This could go really well or really badly!

Matt says that the minister took out a rose, smelt it, stroked its petals, and proceeded to throw it into the crowd. The minister continued with his message and said things like "You don't want syphilis, do you?" and "Everyone is having fun until there's herpes on your lips!" Matt began to wonder exactly what this guy was doing and was very concerned.

Eventually, the minister asked for his rose back. A student came running to the platform with the rose and the rose was broken up, petals were hanging on by a thread, and the minister held it up and asked, "Now who would want this? Who would want this rose!?"

What this minister was pretty much saying is if you sleep around with so many people, or pass yourself around from person to person, no one will ever want you. This was probably birthed out of the purity culture that made sex the most evil of all sins. Events and books were written in such a condemning way that whoever lost their virginity was deemed untouchable and apparently to this guy, irredeemable. The attitude was this: You're too messed up. You're unlovable. You are too **damaged** to ever be wanted again. Just wait until you look a guy or girl in their face and say, "I'm not a virgin" and they will drop you like a bad habit.

Matt says that anger began to swell within his heart and his blood boiled because it took everything inside of him not to scream out to this man that "**Jesus wants the rose**! That's the point of the gospel! That He who knew no sin became sin so that we may have the righteousness of God!" [7]

Essentially what the super religious were saying in this story of the woman caught in adultery, was that her life was not worth saving. Her life was damaged and there was no restoring it. She had too many broken petals and was too messed up. She deserved to die. Just like this minister believed that the rose was no longer worth anything. It deserved to lay dead. But Jesus flips that script. Jesus makes the dead rise again. Jesus wants the rose.

Regardless of what you have done or where you have been abandoned or abused or betrayed, Jesus wants you! Jesus desires to bring you back from death! Jesus sees a soul to be saved! Jesus sees a person to be loved!

I want to remind you that in Jesus, you are no longer damaged, you are delivered. I don't care what others say about you, or what rumor is spread about you, or how chaotic your life has been. Even if you made some bad decisions. Even if you are marked by scars you caused. Jesus STILL loves you because He went to the cross for you! Jesus died so that you can be delivered from the constant pain of shame and guilt.

And remember from the quote at the beginning of the chapter:

Guilt says you made a mistake.
Shame says you are a mistake.
Grace says you are FORGIVEN!

Reflect:

1. If you have ever faced a self-righteous bully, describe that time and how it made you feel.

2. Shame is a prison. Do you believe Jesus can open the prison and let you out of your shame? If so, what's stopping you from walking out of the cell?

3. Think back to this woman caught in adultery: How would you feel if you were caught in an act of sin and dragged and exposed in front of everyone? Have you ever brought someone else's sin to the table? What label did you give them?

4. Who is someone in your life right now that you need to turn compassion on and turn off condemnation?

PART 2
FROM OVERLOOKED
TO CHOSEN

CHAPTER 3

WHAT DOES GOD SEE?

"If you live for people's acceptance,
you'll die from their rejection."
Lecrae

I love proving people wrong. It feels so good and fulfilling to be told you can't do something or won't do something, and then you actually do it and see the haters' reactions. When you can work hard and hustle to become what you believe you are called to do, all people can do is talk while you shine.

When I was in 8th grade, I played basketball for a local Christian school in Monroe, Louisiana. To be honest, I was decent. I had the hustle, the desire, the work ethic, and raw talent. But I was definitely missing fundamentals and confidence to really play basketball at my full potential. However, after talking with the varsity coach, I was allowed to go out and practice with the varsity team.

Now of course, what I discovered was that even if my brother Daniel did play for this varsity basketball team, rarely do any upperclassmen enjoy having a middle schooler around. But I was hungry, and at some level, I didn't really care what they thought. I wanted to ball!

I remember one practice specifically because it was scrimmage day. And even though, as a ballplayer, drills and different workouts are fun, there is nothing like getting on the court and showing others the baller in you.

However, there were certain players that weren't having it. Knowing full well that I was involved in every aspect of the day's practice, the captain of the team came up to me and told me "Don't expect to play at all." I remember thinking: "What a jerk!" But I decided to pass on his comment because I wanted to play!

Right when the coach told us to get to the sidelines for him to pick teams, I zoomed to the front. I wanted to play in the game! I wanted to display my raw talent and take these dudes on! I'm telling you, I was like Rudy: too small, scrappy, skill not even close to any of the player's level, worked my tail off, and was ready to get in the game at a moment's notice.

While I am at the front of the line of all of these JV and varsity players, I feel a tug on my jersey. I was pulled back to the back of the huddle. Like I was some dog being grabbed by a leash because I was going after a squirrel. I looked to the side, and sure enough, it was the jerk captain pulling me to the back only to reiterate, "Don't expect to play today."

He walked away like it was some drop the mic moment. Like it was some display of leadership that paved the way to put me in my place as an 8th grader. There was not one player that had my back out there. There was not an ounce of respect for even the hustle that I knew they saw in me.

Sometimes according to the world's standards, no one respects the hustle until you produce results. But how could I produce results without the chance to play? So you know what I ultimately felt? Do you know what deep down inside was screaming at me from that moment on? This one word or label overwhelmed me:

Overlooked.

That moment before the basketball scrimmage brought out insecurities I didn't know I had. To this day, that moment has made me feel like there is always going to be someone pulling me back from what I believe is my dream and maybe even my destiny. When you feel overlooked, you start believing that you will always have to prove yourself and scout for affirmation from others.

I am positive that I am not the only one who has felt or been overlooked. It's a part of life. In a world of status, popularity, pride, and brokenness there will never be a moment when people don't feel overlooked, underrated, undervalued, and insignificant.

But I will say this - you are in good company. Even the greatest in the history of humanity have been overlooked.

Let's take a look at God's word on the matter. Let's look at a man whose name was David.

The story comes out of 1 Samuel 16. Grab your Bible and let's check it out.

Before we dive into the verses let me sum up what's going on:

Let's talk about Saul. This is not New Testament Saul, though we WILL address that Saul later.

This is Saul from the Old Testament. He is the king of Israel who was anointed by the Prophet Samuel. He is the king that God gave to His people who weren't satisfied with God being God. They wanted a physical presence to rule. They demanded it!

Saul was the kind of king that did what he wanted, who was tall and handsome, and had status and power. He was described as being head and shoulders taller than everyone.

Saul was a people pleaser as well and feared people over fearing God.
The Prophet Samuel delivered the news to Saul that one day he would be replaced because he "rejected the word of the Lord."

Samuel grieved Saul though after his many failures.

Let's read it:

The Lord said to Samuel, "How long are you going to mourn for Saul, since I have rejected him as king over Israel? Fill your horn with oil and go. *I am sending you to Jesse of Bethlehem because I have selected for myself a king from his sons."*
2 Samuel asked, "How can I go? Saul will hear about it and kill me!"

The Lord answered, "Take a young cow with you and say, 'I have come to sacrifice to the Lord.' 3 Then invite Jesse to the sacrifice, and I will let you know what you are to do. *You are to anoint for me the one I indicate to you."*

4 Samuel did what the Lord directed and went to Bethlehem. When the elders of the town met him, they trembled and asked, "Do you come in peace?"

5 "In peace," he replied. "I've come to sacrifice to the Lord. Consecrate yourselves and come with me to the sacrifice." Then he consecrated Jesse and his sons and invited them to the sacrifice. 6 When they arrived, *Samuel saw Eliab and said, "Certainly the Lord's anointed one is here before him."*

7 But the Lord said to Samuel, *"Do not look at his appearance or his stature because I have rejected him. Humans do not see what the Lord sees, for humans see what is visible, but the Lord sees the heart."*

8 Jesse called Abinadab and presented him to Samuel. "The Lord hasn't chosen this one either," Samuel said. 9 Then Jesse presented Shammah, but Samuel said, "The Lord hasn't chosen this one either." 10 After Jesse presented seven of his sons to him, Samuel told Jesse, "The Lord hasn't chosen any of these." 11 Samuel asked him, "Are these all the sons you have?"

"There is still the youngest," he answered, *"but right now he's tending the sheep."* Samuel told Jesse, "Send for him. We won't sit down to eat until he gets here." 12 So Jesse sent for him. He had beautiful eyes and a healthy, handsome appearance.

Then the Lord said, *"Anoint him, for he is the one."* 13 So Samuel took the horn of oil and anointed him

in the presence of his brothers, and the Spirit of the Lord came powerfully on David from that day forward. Then Samuel set out and went to Ramah.

 -- 1 Samuel 16:1-13 (CSB)

This is where we meet young David. The shepherd boy. The runt of the litter, right?

David was overlooked.

This is the guy who is described as a man after God's own heart!
You see, sometimes we already know a man or woman's status before we know their history. Their "come up" as we would say. We all label them as successes and failures without knowing the behind the scenes.

Well truthfully, David was labeled by everyone else before he knew he was actually the chosen one.

I want you to think about three principles that I believe God reveals in this passage:

Number one: **Appearance doesn't *reveal* what people are really like or what their *value* is.**

Look back at verses 6-7:

6 When they arrived, Samuel saw Eliab and said, "Certainly the Lord's anointed one is here before him." 7 But the Lord said to Samuel, *"Do not look at his appearance or his stature because I have rejected him. Humans do not see what the Lord sees, for humans see what is visible, but the Lord sees the heart."* **-- 1 Samuel 16:6-7 (CSB)**

Samuel at this moment saw Eliab and assumed he would be the chosen king. We assume this is why Samuel said, "**certainly this is him**!" Because Samuel was used to the stature of Saul, internally he may have believed God was looking for someone similar in appearance.

But God didn't have a face in mind, he had a heart in mind. Mel Gibson's character in Braveheart, William Wallace says, "People don't follow titles, they follow courage." [1] Maybe Samuel didn't realize that just because someone looks the part or has great stature, doesn't mean they are automatically a leader. But that's how we think sometimes, isn't it?

Maybe David would have been overlooked because his brothers were taller and more handsome. But remember as God told Samuel, **"Do not look at his appearance or stature because I have rejected him. Humans do not see what the Lord sees, for humans see what is visible, but the Lord sees the heart."**

As you read this right now, maybe you can relate:

- You posted a photo and an inspirational quote or something motivating and people overlooked it. So, you decided it was not pretty enough. But no one can see your true heart on social media.
- You are on the team, but coaches and players wonder if you are tall enough or strong enough to play at all, even though you've been working harder than anyone and you value the discipline it takes. *See my story at the beginning of this chapter.*
- You crave to be authentically you, but the crew that you want to be a part of expects you to be someone else, dress in a certain style, and they put pressure on you to be like them. **You are not worthy unless you change.**

Sometimes we can have it all together visibly, yet still be invisible. Our hearts matter. I've heard students and adults alike say, "I just want someone to see me."

Regardless if people SEE you or not, ask this question: **Who** does God see??

It doesn't matter what people say or see when you have the love and affection of the king!

I want you to hear this: **The Lord sees you and He wants your heart.**

Number two: **God's approval > man's approval.**

11 Samuel asked him, "Are these all the sons you have?" "There is still the youngest," he answered, "but right now he's tending the sheep." Samuel told Jesse, "Send for him. We won't sit down to eat until he gets here." 12 So Jesse sent for him. He had beautiful eyes and a healthy, handsome appearance. Then the Lord said, "Anoint him, for he is the one." **-- 1 Samuel 16:11-12 (CSB)**

One of my favorite quotes that stays in my head daily is at the beginning of the chapter title:

"If you live for people's acceptance, you'll die from their rejection." - Lecrae [2]

For a lot of us, people's opinions are an idol. We crave it, we want it, and when we get it we're good. But when it is not there, we feel like losers. So, we take on the labels of overlooked and loser.

I watched a Right Now Media Bible series on Ephesians taught by J.D. Greear, and he gave this incredible analogy based on the show, **The Voice.** The premise of the show is that the singing coaches hear the contestants sing, but they face away from the stage and don't get to watch the performance. If more than one coach pushes their button for the same person, that contestant gets the chance to choose who they want to work with. If none of the coaches push their button, the contestant is **eliminated**.

But here is the beauty of the gospel: *Even before you walked this earth, before you said a word, or even before you could discover your talent...**Jesus hit the button...and chose you!**[3]*

Even when others don't choose you, God chooses you!

Just like David, you don't need man's approval when you have God's anointing!

While his father and brothers just saw a shepherd boy. God saw a king!

Number three: **people's opinions of you can't mess up the opportunities God has chosen for you.**

12 So Jesse sent for him. He had beautiful eyes and a healthy, handsome appearance. Then the Lord said, "Anoint him, for he is the one." 13 So Samuel took the horn of oil and anointed him in the presence of his brothers, and the Spirit of the Lord came powerfully on David from that day forward. Then Samuel set out and went to Ramah. -- 1 Samuel 16:12-13 (CSB)

David was anointed. This means he was set apart for a divine purpose, to be used by God.

Look at David's resume!

David is in the lineage of Jesus.
David killed bears and lions with bare hands and overcame the 9-foot-giant Goliath.
David became a king!
David wrote 73 of the 150 Psalms in your Bible.
David had the power of the Spirit upon him.

Well, Griff, I don't know if God will ever use me to do things that big!

Why not??? Are you trusting man, or God? Don't tell God what he can't do!
If God wants you to be somewhere, he will get you there.
But your heart has to be his. Your heart has to believe you are chosen...not overlooked

The label you need to rip off: **Overlooked**
The truth to embrace: **You are chosen.**

Back to my story about being an overlooked 8th-grade basketball player.
I kept working. I not only kept working but I would eventually outwork every player on the varsity team.
Most of them played in the game when it was time to

play, but they didn't work off the court when no one was watching. They were too caught up in status, pursuing girls, being class clowns, and losing. I think they won 10 games and lost 25 that year. But I digress...maybe.

I would eventually leave that school because the labels put on me from a school worsened, in my opinion. I didn't fit in and just didn't have any really good friends. I hated it there. And internally, I knew I was not going to get better as a ballplayer if I stayed. So, I left.

I played AAU travel basketball. I was playing against high-level talent and I got better. Instead of getting pushed to the back by an insecure captain, I was challenged to keep getting better. There was no one trying to pull me away. I ended up transitioning to a new high school towards the end of my 8th-grade year. This school had one of the premier basketball teams in the state, so I would be transferring from an "Ok" basketball school to "this is what we major in as a school" basketball squad. I was ecstatic! And once again, everyone at my former school overlooked me and doubted that I could make the basketball team.

I went to this 5A high school, tried out, and made the team! I started on the freshman team and played a lot for the JV team. What's even cooler is I was able to go back and scrimmage against all of the guys who doubted me.

And if I could brag for a moment: They couldn't stop me! The hard work, the rebellion against their disbelief in me, and the talent God gave me, which I kept working on, were displayed that day.

Being overlooked doesn't have to cripple you; it can actually challenge you to realize that you are actually chosen for greatness. No matter what that looks like in your life, greatness is in you. You are an image bearer of the one true God. And when you step into a relationship with Jesus, you realize he is actually the true and better David. Jesus is actually the chosen one who paid the price for our lives. He paid the debt we couldn't pay. And when you place your faith and trust in Jesus, He takes up residence in you through the power of the Holy Spirit and chooses you to be great for his kingdom.

Remember:

God never overlooks you.
God doesn't label you.
God chooses you!

Reflect:

1. Describe a time you were overlooked at some point in your life, whether in the past or currently. Get real about it. Why is this label so crippling?

2. What is a dream you have given up on that God has given you? What dream are you pursuing currently but you are struggling to have confidence because of naysayers? What can you do right now to go after it, by the strength of God?

3. What would your life look like right now if you
    decided to walk in the truth that God loves
    you, sees you, and chooses you? What
    confidence did David walk in?

4. Write a prayer or anthem out right now, that
    you will choose to walk in the confidence and
    assurance of God.

CHAPTER 4
OUR LESS IS
HIS MORE

*"When God has something for you,
it doesn't matter who stands against it"
Chadwick Boseman, Black Panther*

When greatness is decided, greatness cannot be detonated. What I think is incredibly powerful about greatness is that it is not just given, it is earned. What I think we undervalue about greatness is that it is often ordinary people who choose to do extraordinary things that no one else is willing to do. There are many examples of this that have impacted me.

I want to start with boxer Gene Tunney. I read about him in an article by Tim Elmore and then in Tim Elmore's book The Pandemic Population.

Tim's article reads as:

> *"If you've followed professional boxing over the last century, you know the name, Jack Dempsey. Jack was the heavyweight champion of the world for seven years.*

But do you know the name of the guy who beat him?

Probably not. He was a nobody by the name of Gene Tunney. Gene had set a goal as a young man that he wanted to be a professional boxer—until he faced a setback during his military service. Gene broke all of the fingers in both of his hands. His trainer and his doctor both told him he'd have to give up boxing. His brittle bones would not allow it. Gene had a decision in front of him.

Interestingly, Tunney decided he would not give up his goal of being a boxer. In fact, he wanted to be the heavyweight champion of the world. He just changed his methods of preparation. Gene began to learn the art of self-defense, which allowed him to use a different part of his hand for his craft. He learned to run backward, knowing that facing Jack Dempsey he'd have to run backwards a few rounds. He completely changed the way he approached his goal.

And when Gene Tunney finally got his chance to take on Jack Dempsey, he whipped him. It shocked everyone. It so humiliated Jack Dempsey, that Dempsey challenged Tunney to a rematch. Tunney beat him a second time. He was no fluke.

Now here's the truth I want you to catch.

Fistic experts, who understand boxing, tell us something intriguing. They estimate there is no way that Gene Tunney could have beaten Jack Dempsey for the heavyweight crown had he NOT broken all the fingers in both of his hands. No one at the time could go head to head and toe to toe with Dempsey and survive. It was the very setback (even tragedy) Tunney faced that launched him toward his goal.
His setback actually enabled him to come back better."[1]

Gene was labeled a nobody, but he beat a somebody. He was overlooked and his label was an insignificant one, but he became great through perseverance. He was able to turn his setback into a comeback through grit and determination!

Another determined soul I admire is Stephen Curry, the point guard for the Golden State Warriors. There is a story of him being at a Nike Skills Academy with the top 20 high school shooting guards in the nation and the top 10 college guards in the country. This was a skills academy led by the late great Kobe Bryant.

At that time it was said that Stephen Curry was not even the most recognized player there. In other words he was overlooked. Isn't that funny? Can you imagine? You are one of the top 30 players in the country, and they're not even talking or thinking about you. However, the narrator of this story would say what stood out about Curry was his work ethic. Thirty minutes before every practice, which at the time was two a day for three straight days, while every player was still in their flip flops with their headphones on, Curry was already shooting, warming up, practicing game shots, and doing dribbling drills. It was said that right when a workout started, Curry had already made one hundred to one hundred fifty shots and was in a full sweat.

Curry was a perfectionist and would change or adjust his shot if he needed. The narrator said that "*Success is not an accident. Success is a choice*." The daily consistent habits Steph formed informed his future. The Narrator also said, "Are the habits you have today on par with the dreams you have tomorrow?" Determination. Steph is one of the greatest, if not the greatest shooter in basketball today. He went from being overlooked and unrecognized at a camp to one of the most talked about basketball players on the planet.[2]

When you mix what you believe you are destined for with determination, watch out! You might be on the verge of greatness!

Here's the question we need to answer: Did they have doubts? Absolutely! Did they fail? Absolutely! Did they once question their own pursuits? It's hard for me to believe otherwise. It's not that you won't have doubts! You wouldn't be human if you didn't face doubts. But determination is choosing to look those doubts in the face and using them as motivation to prove others wrong and God right. *It's believing that if God has given you a calling he can open the door, and only he can shut the door if it is not meant to be.*

Think about Jeremiah from the Old Testament:

"The words of Jeremiah, the son of Hilkiah, one of the priests living in Anathoth in the territory of Benjamin.
2 The word of the Lord came to him in the thirteenth year of the reign of Josiah son of Amon, king of Judah. 3 It also came throughout the days of Jehoiakim son of Josiah, king of Judah, until the fifth month of the eleventh year of Zedekiah son of Josiah, king of Judah, when the people of Jerusalem went into exile.
4 The word of the Lord came to me:
5 I chose you before I formed you in the womb;
I set you apart before you were born.

**I appointed you a prophet to the nations.
6 But I protested, "Oh no, Lord God! Look, I don't
know how to speak since I am only a youth." --
Jeremiah 1:1-6 (CSB)**

Jeremiah was chosen to stand out and be a prophet.
Yet Jeremiah still shook in fear because of what he
thought was a disqualification: his age! You see, even
this great prophet doubted. You are in good
company there. But remember, if God has destined
you for something great, who can stand against it?

Jeremiah is one of the greatest prophets to ever live
and he brought a lot of emotion to his prophetic role.
This earned him the name, "the weeping prophet."

Tony Evans sums it up well in his Study Bible:

> "As judgment was being prepared for the
> sinful kingdom of Judah through the
> Babylonian Empire Jeremiah was called to
> announce the rightness of that judgment
> because of Judah's great sin against God. His
> daunting task was to bring the message of
> rejection to God's people. But in the midst of
> that, Jeremiah also issued a call to the people
> to repent so that their situation might be
> reversed, and another call to the people who
> would not be taken into captivity in Babylon
> to repent so that things would not become
> worse. God commanded Jeremiah not to

marry as an illustration of the isolation God was feeling from his sinful people. And yet, it is in Jeremiah that God reveals a new kingdom covenant he would make with his people to cleanse them, give them new hearts, and restore them to him. The good news of Jeremiah is that despite our sin, God offers us restoration if we will repent and return to him." [3]

Jeremiah had protested God because he labeled himself too young or inadequate. But what is so cool about God is his ability to demonstrate his power in human weakness.

Jeremiah needed to hear what I always tell teenagers: *You are NEVER too young to make an impact and have influence.* It's a choice. And it is a belief that God is bigger.

Even in the face of a lot of rejection, Jeremiah would remain faithful to God through his prophetic voice. His destiny and determination collided with the will of God! And he has a book named after him in the Old Testament of God's word!

I think of another guy by the name of Gideon in the book of Judges chapters 6-8. Gideon was called upon to save the people of Israel by leading them against the Midianites. In a commonly used phrase among the people of Israel, they had done "what was evil in the sight of the Lord, and the Lord gave them into the hand of Midian."

The Midianites were capturing all the crops produced by the Israelites they could, giving them a rough time. When the people of Israel realized their wicked ways, they cried out for help to the Lord. So, God sent a prophet to deliver them, just as they had been rescued from Egypt.

So God appoints Gideon!
When Gideon was harvesting wheat and hiding from the Midianites, an angel spoke to him:

11 The angel of the Lord came, and he sat under the oak that was in Ophrah, which belonged to Joash, the Abiezrite. His son Gideon was threshing wheat in the winepress in order to hide it from the Midianites. 12 Then the angel of the Lord appeared to him and said, "The Lord is with you, valiant warrior." -- Judges 6:11-12 (CSB)

Gideon was being cowardly, but that was not his identity. Gideon was scared but he would soon realize God had other plans for him. The angel told Gideon that God is sending him to "save Israel from the hand of Midian." Although at first Gideon doubts his ability to accomplish this mighty task, he takes heart because God would be with him in this mission. God Called Gideon "Valiant Warrior" and gave him a new label!

First, Gideon is commanded to destroy the Altar of Baal that the Israelites constructed, evidence of their disbelief. At night time, Gideon and ten of his men took down the altar of Baal. This ticked the townspeople off and had them asking for the death of the altar destroyer. Joash, the father of Gideon, then tells them if Baal really is a god he will kill Gideon himself, saving his son.

Seeking reassurance from the Lord, Gideon asks God to prove His promise to save Israel, using a fleece. Inspired by the mighty acts of God, Gideon and his men then travel near the camp of Midian and prepare for a fight.

But what God did would come as a shock to Gideon. God wanted the Israelites to realize his divine power, so He commanded Gideon to lessen his army from thousands to just 300 men to defeat the Midianites.

2 The Lord said to Gideon, "You have too many troops for me to hand the Midianites over to them, or else Israel might elevate themselves over me and say, 'I saved myself.' -- Judges 7:2 (CSB)

Can you imagine being given thousands of warriors to fight with, only for God to decrease it? I would personally be frustrated and believe that my army would be weak! "God, why would you dwindle my army down?"

Have you ever felt so weak that you question God's provision for you?
You believe God is dwindling your resources and it starts to make your situation look worse?

But what if God is doing it *on* purpose *for* a purpose?

God didn't want Gideon's army, or Gideon himself, to label themselves the mighty men who got the victory. So, God kept dwindling the army down.

God could do more with hundreds than Gideon could do with thousands.
God can always do more with less than we can do with an abundance.

But of course, God gives a promise:

The Lord said to Gideon, "I will deliver you with the three hundred men who lapped and hand the Midianites over to you. But everyone else is to go home." 8 So Gideon sent all the Israelites to their tents but kept the three hundred troops, who took the provisions and their rams' horns. The camp of Midian was below him in the valley. -- Judges 7:7-8 (CSB)

Gideon overhears from a dream of a Midianite that he is destined to conquer Midian and save the Israelites from oppression.

13 When Gideon arrived, there was a man telling his friend about a dream. He said, "Listen, I had a dream: a loaf of barley bread came tumbling into the Midianite camp, struck a tent, and it fell. The loaf turned the tent upside down so that it collapsed." -- Judges 7:13 (CSB)

The story keeps getting better!

God tells Gideon:

"Get up, for the Lord has handed the Midianite camp over to you." Judges 7:15 (CSB).

In order to accomplish something great, he had to keep walking in the presence of God.

Gideon says to the army,

17 "Watch me," he said to them, "and do what I do. When I come to the outpost of the camp, do as I do. 18 When I and everyone with me blow our rams' horns, you are also to blow your rams' horns all around the camp. Then you will say, 'For the Lord and for Gideon!'"

19 Gideon and the hundred men who were with him went to the outpost of the camp at the beginning of the middle watch after the sentries had been stationed. They blew their rams' horns

and broke the pitchers that were in their hands. 20 The three companies blew their rams' horns and shattered their pitchers. They held their torches in their left hands and their rams' horns to blow in their right hands, and they shouted, "A sword for the Lord and for Gideon!" 21 Each Israelite took his position around the camp, and the entire Midianite army began to run, and they cried out as they fled. 22 When Gideon's men blew their three hundred rams' horns, the Lord caused the men in the whole army to turn on each other with their swords. They fled to Acacia House in the direction of Zererah as far as the border of Abel-meholah near Tabbath. 23 Then the men of Israel were called from Naphtali, Asher, and Manasseh, and they pursued the Midianites. -- Judges 7:17-23 (CSB)

Gideon is given the victory with 300 warriors!

I love this question that gives us perspective, "Did the army dwindle? Was it weak? Or was God about to work?"

Feel this: **You have a destiny, and even if you are relentlessly determined, you need God to work.**

Our success is weak when we don't allow God to work.
Our resources are weak when we forget God can make something out of nothing.

What are your dreams? What big thing do you want to accomplish?

You can be overlooked by everyone but still be seen and used by the only one that matters. His name is Jesus, and he chooses you!

Are you walking with Him?

Rip off the label of inadequacy and walk in the security God gives you!

Let me give you Three steps before you reflect:

1. *Get over what people think about you*: Caring about what people think is not worth your mental health or your soul. People are going to overlook you. You cannot control what people think about you. That's a full-time job that is not worth the pay.

2. *Keep shining your light even when others try to dim it:* God has too bright a future for you to hide your light just because others can't stand it. When others try to throw a sheet over you, dodge it boldly and confidently. You might blind others with your light, but there are still a bunch of people you will guide with your light.

3. *Keep looking inward (at yourself), upward (at God), and outward (to influence people)*: God

has no limits to what he can do through your influence. Always reflect inwardly. Always look up to God for intimacy and guidance. Always choose to impact and influence those who actually believe you have something to say.

Reflect:

1. Do you believe you have a bright future? Is there anything you are working towards right now that will not be easy? Explain.

2. In order to rip off the overlooked label, you must be honest about your circumstances: Do you have all that you need in Christ Jesus or are you worried about your resources dwindling?

3. Describe a time where you were doubted because of external circumstances. Did you also doubt yourself? What if doubting your own strength is good? What if it means God is about to work?

4. Name something you have accomplished because of God's strength. Now, if he did it then, why wouldn't He do it again?

INTERLUDE
WORRY

"The Lord is a warrior; the Lord is his name." - Exodus 15:3

I want to go ahead and spill the news to you. I have another book I am working on. Not sure when it will be published, but it's a work in progress for sure.

It's called 'When Panic Attacks'. It is my story and my strategy on how I fight worry. It's also me at my most transparent and authentic self. I desire to help you know how to fight when panic attacks. I tell you that to tell you this: YOU are NOT a WORRIER.

When it comes to labels, we must be very careful how we say what or who we are. By now you have discovered some lies that we have placed on ourselves or lies that have been placed on us by others, but without a doubt lies God never gave us. Words have power over our lives, so it matters what we say and how we say it.

Truthfully, though I struggle big time with anxiety and worry, I will never say "I AM a worrier." I AM an anxious person." The reason that I don't say those things is because I know, through the power of Jesus and his intense authority, I will defeat it one day. I know one day, by his power, I will stop taking the anxiety medicine I'm on. By his power, I will spit worry out the window like chewed-up gum because it will no longer be something I sit in chew on but something I will get rid of quickly.

I am not there yet, to be honest.
But one thing I thought about the other day is that I allow worry to master me. When I do tell myself lies like "I am a worrier! I am worthless! I suck!" I am allowing worry to master me.
If I can keep it all the way real with you: I am essentially saying "I am my thoughts. I am my burden. I do suck at this. I am not able." In this moment, Satan has me exactly where he wants me: Me being my own worst enemy.

But – Satan as an enemy, and me as an enemy, is no match for the ultimate warrior that is God!
The label I must rip off is "I am a worrier. Worry is my master."

What I must preach to myself on a daily basis is this:

"Worry is not my master and Jesus is my savior!

When I say this out loud, I feel empowered. I feel like a beast. Why? Because Jesus has intense authority and my thoughts must bow to Him. My worry must bow to the intense authority Jesus has.

Worry makes me miserable while Jesus makes me joyful.
Worry makes me think evil and jacked up thoughts while Jesus loves on me.
Worry disables me and makes me depressed while Jesus empowers me and gives me rest.
Worry fills me with the pride that, "I must handle it" while Jesus humbles me and says, "I already handled it!"
Worry makes me sick while Jesus heals my soul.

Here's my question: Who is your savior?

It's time to rip off the label of "I am a worrier" and replace it with "My God is a warrior!"
And because my God is a warrior and that warrior lives in me, I can win the war against worry!
Worry is a horrible liar, and my God is a great savior!

PART 3
FROM A FORMER LIFE
TO A FAITHFUL LIFE

CHAPTER 5
NEVER TOO FAR GONE

"We had to celebrate and rejoice, because this brother of yours was dead and is alive again; he was lost and is found." -- The Father in the Parable of the Lost Son.

I was living in Simpson, Louisiana, for a season, as a youth pastor and I also started to volunteer as the assistant basketball coach at Simpson High School. It was a great season of ministry in this small but close-knit community. I was what they called a big city boy in the country. It was cool to see if context was really king when it comes to reaching people with the gospel! Ha, I didn't speak anything like these country boys and girls. I was this ghetto cajun white dude who didn't hunt or fish, but I did play basketball and listened to hip hop. And those two registered well!

I remember my first Wednesday night speaking to the student ministry when I met a small family. There was a mom and her two boys, Greg and Daniel. Greg was very shy but also a smiley person. Daniel was very quiet and dressed in what we call gothic clothes. Now, I only say that to paint a picture for you. It didn't bother me one bit that he wore all black, had chains on, and whatnot. I was just pumped up to meet them. The mom was very friendly and they were excited about me becoming the new youth pastor.

However, every Wednesday night over the summer, Greg always showed up to our student worship service, but I never saw Daniel. From what I had heard from the mom, Greg, and others, Daniel was not the church kind of guy. He was also what I heard an atheist and at one point in his life a satanist. This is what I heard his label was.

Later that year, I was walking into the gym for basketball practice and I ran right into Daniel. Like, I merely opened the door and there he was! This is what you call a divine appointment!

"What's up Derek!?" I said, "What up bro! How you been, dude?" I am so glad I asked that question because if there is one thing I have always loved about Daniel is his raw honesty.

He wasn't good. Anxiety and depression were eating him alive and he asked if a guy like him could go to church. And it just so happened to be a Wednesday night, when our student worship service was held. I said "Bro you better come, and we would be pumped up for a guy like you to come to church! You see Daniel had labeled himself, "A guy like me." As in, "I would hate to corrupt your church."

This stuff always makes me laugh because what kind of culture have we created Church to be? "Come as you are but it better be to our standards." A women once told my mom, "You should come to Sunday School! And you can come as you are honey!" And I loved what my mom asked next, "If I come as I am, can I cuss?" The lady responded, "Well, no, we umm...no of course we couldn't allow that." Come as you are as long as you meet our standards. Apparently, God cannot handle cussing.

So of course, Daniel showed up. And he didn't "corrupt" the Church because we all already do that. I don't care how nicely pressed your Church clothes are, you are still jacked up. I know a lot of "give my best on Sunday" Christians who don't give their spouse or kids their best at home. I know many who put their Sunday face on but are very lonely and angry.

Daniel showed up that night with a humble spirit. I could tell he was hungry. Daniel heard the gospel that night as we were dissecting Ephesians, and I observed him as I preached. He listened. He heard. He leaned in.

Daniel poked me on the shoulder not long after we were done with tears in his eyes. He told me things he had done and the life he had been living currently, and he knew how empty it was making him feel. His dad was not really present in his life and he was in need of a Father who loved him. THAT night, Daniel received Christ as Lord and Savior. The first night he had shown up in a long time. All because we ran into each other at Simpson High School.

He no longer wanted to live in the old self because Jesus had made him new. Daniel's new walk of life became almost immediate. We started hanging out a lot. He got a new Bible and started reading it. He was becoming so devout and studying and loving people well. Daniel started sharing Jesus with friends at school, and later on, students in our ministry started looking up to him for prayer and leadership. There was a light and magnetism about this new found believer in Jesus. It is still to this day one of the most beautiful transformations I have ever seen. His label of his former life was over, and he started to live a faithful one because of Jesus.

There are a lot of people in this world who let their past or what they have done keep them crippled from moving forward. In a very anxious generation, it can be difficult to get over the disgusting things you have done. It can be a frustrating feeling like your identity is caught up in what you have done and you just can't move on.
You begin to assume you are not loveable, cherishable, or even redeemable.

Maybe your past is serious.
Maybe in your mind, your past is spotless compared to most.

Our problem is not only that we can't get over our past, it's when we choose to live and dwell there. Time moves forward. It's actually illogical to live in the past when every second the future begins.

Let me ask you this: *What's the description of your past? Is it in this list of labels below?*

Addict
Anxious
Bully
Arrogant
Bitter
Depressed
Lustful
Broken
Sleep Around
Abused
Abuser
Self-harmer
Never Cussed Before
Never Seen Porn
Always at Church
Memorized Scripture.
Church Kid.

Even though you know what you have done in your past and you would like to move on, people still may define you by what you have done. You are crippled and even struggle to love yourself. Your past terrorizes you. How can a good God know your label while also forgiving and loving you?

Maybe you have always been a good person and there's a self-righteousness about you. You haven't done what others have done, so how can you possibly be that bad? But underneath your cover, there are sins galore that you are ashamed of. If anyone found them out, you'd be dead to them. If they only knew the wicked thoughts you actually thought, no one would give an ear to hear what you have to say.

I want to show you a man who most would assume was too far gone from the grace of God. And if you are a person who compares what you have done to others, I'm sure this man's story and transformation will also empower you to rip off the label of your former way of living.

His name was Saul. We are no longer talking about Old Testament Saul. If you are familiar with the New Testament, then long story short, this man named Saul later becomes a man named Paul. We will get more descriptive there in a bit. But Paul talks about his past in his letter to the Galatians so we can get a brief summary.

13 For you have heard about my <u>former way of life</u> in Judaism: I intensely persecuted God's church and tried to destroy it. -- Galatians 1:13 (CSB)

Saul legitimately believed he was doing God's will by leading revolts to persecute and destroy anyone who believed in Jesus. Saul was what I call the biblical equivalent to today's ISIS or Taliban leader. So he was the overseer of a lot of murders of those who followed Jesus.

Paul also says this:

14 I advanced in Judaism beyond many contemporaries among my people, because I was extremely zealous for the traditions of my ancestors. -- Galatians 1:14 (CSB)

In his letter to the Church at Philippi he says this:

If anyone else thinks he has grounds for confidence in the flesh, I have more: 5 circumcised the eighth day; of the nation of Israel, of the tribe of Benjamin, a Hebrew born of Hebrews; regarding the law, a Pharisee; 6 regarding zeal, persecuting the church; regarding the righteousness that is in the law, blameless. -- Philippians 3:4-6 (CSB)

Saul knew it all! Saul actually was pretty clean and devout in doing "good things."
He had the whole Torah memorized.

He was zealous for good works and displaying good works.

Now let's look back at when Saul comes on the scene. Saul had just approved of the death of the first Christian martyr, Stephen. And he couldn't even come close to predicting what Jesus was about to do in his life.

1 Now Saul was still breathing threats and murder against the disciples of the Lord. He went to the high priest
2 and requested letters from him to the synagogues in Damascus, so that if he found any men or women who belonged to the Way, he might bring them as prisoners to Jerusalem.
3 As he traveled and was nearing Damascus, a light from heaven suddenly flashed around him. 4 Falling to the ground, he heard a voice saying to him, "Saul, Saul, why are you persecuting me?"

5 "Who are you, Lord?" Saul said.

"I am Jesus, the one you are persecuting," he replied. 6 "But get up and go into the city, and you will be told what you must do."

7 The men who were traveling with him stood speechless, hearing the sound but seeing no one. 8 Saul got up from the ground, and though his eyes were open, he could see nothing. So they took him by the hand and led him into Damascus. 9 He was unable to see for three days and did not eat or drink. -- Acts 9:1-9 (CSB)

11 "Get up and go to the street called Straight," the Lord said to him, "to the house of Judas, and ask for a man from Tarsus named Saul, since he is praying there. 12 In a vision he has seen a man named Ananias coming in and placing his hands on him so that he may regain his sight."

13 "Lord," Ananias answered, "I have heard from many people about this man, how much harm he has done to your saints in Jerusalem. 14 And he has authority here from the chief priests to arrest all who call on your name."

15 But the Lord said to him, "Go, for this man is my chosen instrument to take my name to Gentiles, kings, and Israelites. 16 I will show him how much he must suffer for my name." -- Acts 9:1-16 (CSB)

Saul went from being dead to being alive. He went from being lost to being found.
Jesus wrecked shop on Saul's soul and changed him into someone new! And Jesus sends a man to get this dude's discipleship started!

Can you imagine being asked to awaken a killer? Ananias had definitely heard Saul's history. So the fact that God is now calling him to wake up the revolt leader against Christians, I would be like "Lord, send someone else!" What Ananias doesn't understand is this was Saul's history and not his current state, because of what Jesus has done to transform him. Ananias knew a chapter of Saul's life but didn't know the dramatic experience Saul had just had.

The story of Saul's former life defining him continues:

Saul was with the disciples in Damascus for some time. **20 Immediately he began proclaiming Jesus in the synagogues: "He is the Son of God."**

21 All who heard him were astounded and said, "Isn't this the man in Jerusalem who was causing havoc for those who called on this name and came here for the purpose of taking them as prisoners to the chief priests?"

22 But Saul grew stronger and kept confounding the Jews who lived in Damascus by proving that Jesus is the Messiah. -- Acts 9:20-22 (CSB)

Again, Saul is trying to walk in his new life, but those who know his description wanted nothing to do with him. Even the Jews tried to kill him because he left his occupation of revolting against Christians! Saul at this point could not win!

Have you ever felt like you've needed to constantly prove yourself to others, so they can see that you are not who you used to be??

But then finally, a friend drops in:

26 When he arrived in Jerusalem, he tried to join the disciples, but they were all afraid of him, since they did not believe he was a disciple. 27 Barnabas, however, took him and brought him to the apostles and explained to them how Saul had seen the Lord on the road and that the Lord had talked to him, and how in Damascus he had spoken boldly in the name of Jesus. 28 Saul was coming and going with them in Jerusalem, speaking boldly in the name of the Lord. -- Acts 9:26-28 (CSB)

Barnabas endorses Saul! It took a friend to bring to the disciples' attention that this man had indeed been changed. Do you have friends like that?

Barnabas' name actually means "Son of encouragement."
This man believed Saul and had seen the transformation and endorsed him because of it. Do you have a friend like this who looks past your past?

Saul would even be given a new name.

Saul represented his former life...Paul represented his faithful life.

Paul's life became beautiful. I love what N.T. Wright says about Paul in his book, *Paul, A Biography:*

> *"Paul's powerful, spirit-driven proclamation of Jesus as "son of God" can hardly be called "preaching," if by "preaching" we mean the sort of thing that goes on in churches week by week in our world. This was a public announcement, like a medieval herald or town crier walking through the streets with a bell, calling people to attention and declaring that a new king had been placed on the throne."*[1]

It's hard to shut a person's boldness down when they discover Jesus' bold death and resurrection.

I want to give you three things to think about from this story:

Number one: **Your past has a *description,* but your past does not *define* you.**

You are now defined by who you are in Christ Jesus. That's what this book *Labels* is all about; embracing the truth that Jesus is now your life.[2] Your past points to where you came from, and it is definitely a part of your story, but you are defined by who Christ now says you are: *A Saint!*

Paul would no longer be defined as a murderer.
He would no longer be defined by his accolades and pharisaical background.
Those are just descriptions. He was given a new identity!

No matter where you came from, Jesus wants to move you forward. You no longer fit the description of: Adulterer. Cheater. Stealer. Addict. Blasphemer. Drunk. Horrible mom. Deadbeat dad. Terrible friend. Kill those labels in the name of Jesus.

You are defined as: **Child of God!**

Number two: **You are *never too far gone* to experience the *transforming love of Jesus*!**

Jesus called Saul a chosen instrument! He was transformed! He was baptized! A new creation! Again, for those who compare sins, if a killer can experience the grace and forgiveness of God, why can't you?

How can Jesus forgive a man or woman over what they have done?
Because...

It's not about what you have done, it's about what Jesus has done!

And through the power of Jesus, what you have done, is DONE!

The gospel is: You bring God your worst, and he will give you his best.[3] You bring him sin, he will supply the savior!

Number three: **You have been given a *former life* so that you can now live a *faithful life!***

Paul said in Galatians 1:13 ***"You have HEARD about my former life..."***
Who cares what people have heard? You know the truth on which you stand now!

Feel this: It's hard to see your future when you are staring at your past!

The enemy is always going to remind you of your past description. But I love what artist KB alludes to in his song Not Today Satan: *"If Satan reminds you of your past, remind him of his future."*[4] In other words, you have a better future than the one who is lying to you! All he can do is trash talk.

But what does it mean to have a faithful life?

I'm going to make it as simple as possible. I adapted it from the book *The Three Big Questions Every Teenager is asking.*

The faithful life is your everyday YES to Jesus! [5]

I think too many times we settle for Jesus as only our savior without realizing we don't get a savior without a Lord. He now guides you in everyday life. Being saved by grace through faith is also how you walk in Jesus:

By grace: You will not be perfect, but Jesus now dwells in you and reminds you that you can't out sin his grace. Keep walking in that.
Through Faith: You leap every day into the world trusting Jesus to guide you and trusting Jesus to use you!

This changes everything:

**1 In view of the mercies of God, I urge you to present your bodies as a living sacrifice, holy and pleasing to God; this is your true worship.
2 Do not be conformed to this age, but be transformed by the renewing of your mind, so that you may discern what is the good, pleasing, and perfect will of God. -- Romans 12:1-2 (CSB)**

Remember, you are not who you used to be, you are who God says you are!

Reflect:

1. Describe your past. This is a perfect time to go over your testimony, by yourself or with your small group.

2. Why do we sometimes believe that God could never forgive us for what we have done?

3. Describe what it means to be a child of God. Now, considering you are a child of God, why would he only forgive you once but not once and for all?

4. Like Paul had Barnabas, do you have a friend or friends in your life who can remind you of your status with God, and endorse you to those who don't believe that you have changed?

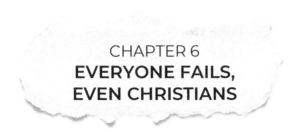

CHAPTER 6
EVERYONE FAILS, EVEN CHRISTIANS

"Perfectionism is a self destructive and addictive belief system that fuels this primary thought: If I look perfect, and do everything perfectly, I can avoid or minimize the painful feelings of shame, judgment, and blame."
— Brené Brown, The Gifts of Imperfection

"Perfectionism is self destructive simply because there's no such thing as perfect. Perfection is an unattainable goal."
— Brené Brown, The Gifts of Imperfection

There is one adjective that I believe describes a lot of us trying to journey through this Christian life: *Exhausted*.

Why are we exhausted? Maybe I can't speak for you, but I can definitely speak for myself and some of the people I know.

We are exhausted trying to chase a label that is unattainable. It is a label we all cognitively know is impossible to gain, but we still strive after it anyways. It is a label that becomes a burden placed on us by others, and ourselves, on a daily basis.

Are you ready?

It's the label of *being perfect*.

Do you know where I struggle with this label? Allow me to be vulnerable with you.

I hate that I am not the best speaker in the world.
I hated when I wasn't the best basketball player in the world.
I hate that as much as I work out I am not the most chiseled or buffest dude ever. I will probably never reach the status of Dwayne Johnson in the arena of fitness. (Maybe I could try steroids??)
I hate that my hair is curly and it isn't pretty boy status like a Zac Efron or Shawn Mendes.
I hate that I am not the best Student Pastor on the planet.

If you ask anyone that has ever known me, especially my precious wife Katie, they will tell you how much insecurity I have felt striving to be the best. This striving for *perfection*.

If something is criticized or critiquing me I get defensive. I always feel like I have to explain myself in all kinds of endeavors. Though I have grown tremendously in this area, it's still a battle!

And I truly believe that if you are like me, it all comes down to this label: *perfection*.
And I am truly *exhausted* chasing it.

Maybe you are reading this and your advice immediately is: "Griff, you will never be perfect! Get over it!"

Okay fair. Thanks for the wisdom.

But ask yourself:

Have you ever seen a Pinterest post of the smiley good looking family and tried to emulate it with yours? And in the process, you got angry with your kids and spouse because it wasn't...perfect? Yeah, you chase perfection.

Have you ever as a boss gotten really fed up with your team because something went awfully wrong? And you were livid because, in the name of excellence, it shouldn't have gone wrong? And even though no one else ever noticed, YOU noticed? Yeah, you chase perfection.

Has your schedule ever been so packed that you actually felt important and useful until you experienced agitation and burn out but you still managed to push forward? And you give you up your peace because you are chasing...perfection?

Have you ever gotten mad at a one-year-old for not understanding your desire for him or her to smash a cake like you saw other moms and dads do? And you're frustrated that...again a one-year-old...didn't comprehend what you wanted them to do? So, you waste energy and time...because you want perfection?

Have you ever denied taking anxiety or depression pills because you would look unfaithful to God and others would judge you? Yeah, I've been there.

And when has any of these things above ever actually made you perfect? How many of these scenarios above have ever cost you something that you weren't wanting to give up?

You are exhausted, aren't you?
Be honest with yourself.

As a pastor and spiritual leader, I used to believe I had to maintain and create this "I've got it together" image. Chasing perfection has cost me relationships (both friendships and romantic relationships). I didn't want people to know I struggled. I didn't want people to know I sinned! Because I wanted to be the ultimate, perfect leader. And in the name of "*becoming all things to all people*", people pleasing became my go to.

Some of us can put on a facade around others that we are neat and tidy Christians. We believe we have this huge Christian reputation to protect, and we don't want to make anyone stumble because they see our faults and failures. Being above reproach doesn't mean being this sophisticated, uptight, self-righteous person. Lord have mercy, that's way too exhausting. That's something we created, not Jesus. Trust me, you can dress fancy, pat your heart at the right time in worship, give a lot of money, make sure to not cuss, and you can still be worse than you think.

We can walk in so much freedom by understanding that even though we are in Christ Jesus, we will be hurt. We will hurt others, cuss, say stupid things, rub people the wrong way, and etc.

It's time to rip off that label of perfection.
It's time to stop being exhausted about something that is unattainable.

I am encouraged by a guy named Peter.
Peter was a fisherman and one of Jesus' best friends. And his story is very relatable.

Have you ever known someone who ended up with a foot in their mouth? That was Peter.

Have you ever known a person who said things no one else was saying and did things no one else did? That was Peter.

27 Immediately Jesus spoke to them. "Have courage! It is I. Don't be afraid."

28 "Lord, if it's you," Peter answered him, "command me to come to you on the water."

29 He said, "Come."

And climbing out of the boat, Peter started walking on the water and came toward Jesus. 30 But when he saw the strength of the wind, he was afraid, and beginning to sink he cried out, "Lord, save me!"

31 Immediately Jesus reached out his hand, caught hold of him, and said to him, "You of little faith, why did you doubt?" -- Matthew 14:27-31 (CSB)

Have you ever hung out with a person who could be correct one moment but audaciously wrong in the next?

Look where Peter got it right:

15 "But you," he asked them, "who do you say that I am?"

16 Simon Peter answered, "You are the Messiah, the Son of the living God." -- Matthew 16:15-16 (CSB)

And now look where Peter got a foot shoved in his mouth:

21 From then on Jesus began to point out to his disciples that it was necessary for him to go to Jerusalem and suffer many things from the elders, chief priests, and scribes, be killed, and be raised the third day. 22 Peter took him aside and began to rebuke him, "Oh no, Lord! This will never happen to you!"

23 Jesus turned and told Peter, "Get behind me, Satan! You are a hindrance to me because you're not thinking about God's concerns but human concerns." -- Matthew 16:21-23 (CSB)

If you have ever read through the life of Peter, have you ever been like "Gosh Peter can't ever get it right!" Only to realize that Peter's story is possibly the most relatable story to us all. An imperfect man who tried to follow Jesus the best he could. An imperfect man who even cut off a man's ear to protect Jesus from a fight, not realizing, it was Jesus' fight to lose so that Peter's soul could be saved. [1] An imperfect man who would get caught up in an argument about his greatness because of his association with Jesus.

But I believe the worst moment of Peter's life was the moment he denied Jesus not once, not twice, but three times. Jesus even told Peter that he would do it! He said a rooster would crow the moment he hit the trifecta denial!

Have you ever been told you were going to do something or not do something, but your desire was to prove someone wrong? I feel like the moment Peter was asked about his association with Jesus he might have thought, "No, I'm going to prove Jesus wrong! I will not deny my friend! I am a day-one and a real one!"

69 Now Peter was sitting outside in the courtyard. A servant girl approached him and said, "You were with Jesus the Galilean too."

70 But he denied it in front of everyone: "I don't know what you're talking about."

71 When he had gone out to the gateway, another woman saw him and told those who were there, "This man was with Jesus the Nazarene!"

72 And again he denied it with an oath: "I don't know the man!"

73 After a little while those standing there approached and said to Peter, "You really are one of them, since even your accent gives you away."

74 Then he started to curse and to swear with an oath, "I don't know the man!" Immediately a rooster crowed, 75 and Peter remembered the words Jesus had spoken, "Before the rooster crows, you will deny me three times." And he went outside and wept bitterly. -- Matthew 26:69-75 (CSB)

Put yourself in Peter's shoes at THIS moment.
Jesus looks at Peter after his bold denial.
And Peter sinks into grief, guilt, and shame.

75 and Peter remembered the words Jesus had spoken, "Before the rooster crows, you will deny me three times." And he went outside and wept bitterly. -- Matthew 26:75

There have been many moments when I have failed and wept bitterly and disgustingly over my sin. There have been times in my life when I have lost my appetite for weeks over shame and guilt. There's something about being awfully wrong and caught in the turmoil of something you caused that hits you in the gut. This is honestly not a bad thing though. If I had no remorse for my sin, no desire for repentance, I would question my own salvation.

If you have never been there, you either haven't lived long enough or haven't lived hard enough. Imperfection finds us out sooner than later. Peter legitimately thought he wouldn't do the very thing he did: *Deny his best friend.* Peter was not perfect. Peter was not the ultimate being. He was not a superhuman. When the pressure was on, he failed. He rejected the man who had led and guided him for three and a half years.

You have been there, right?

If you are in the faith and follow Jesus, there have been times you have denied Jesus.
You took on the label "*Jesus Denier*".

You chose to look at porn over spending time in prayer. Jesus denied.
You chose to cheat on your spouse over keeping the covenant. Jesus denied.
You chose to use your power for abuse and greed. Jesus denied.
You took a gamble on something that wasn't holy and you lost dramatically. Jesus denied.
You chose to show up to Church every Sunday, dressed in your best, worshipping God, but still harbored bitterness towards a friend or family member that you knew needed your forgiveness, but you wouldn't give it. Jesus denied.

You chose to remain a virgin all your life until you met the one that you wanted to marry, but you slept with them and ruined the entire relationship. Jesus denied.

Maybe none of these scenarios represent you, but can you think for a moment of examples like this where you denied him?

Here is what all of this means: *You are not perfect and you will fail miserably. You will never be a perfect Christian. You should get over that now.*

But that doesn't mean you should label yourself a failure.
Denying Jesus doesn't mean you lost your salvation.
Denying Jesus at any moment means we chose something lesser over him!
Peter demonstrated this.
But you need to feel this and speak this over your life when you are exhausted by perfection: **There are always opportunities to turn back to Jesus!**

Because when we bring our imperfections to Jesus, He reminds us of His perfection!

I want you to read this quote that I saw the other day on Instagram from my friend Stuart Hall:

"Failure is a bruise, not a tattoo. Stop acting as if something temporary is permanent."

That is so freeing. We create failure as permanent when we beat ourselves up constantly for something we did. We can even let the effects linger for years. But this is not Jesus' desire for you.

I have been that Jesus denier. I have labeled myself a complete failure!
But when I remember the salvation Jesus gave me, and remember the way he died to set me free, it frees me to walk in my imperfections because God sees Jesus in me!

23 For all have sinned and fall short of the glory of God; 24 they are justified freely by his grace through the redemption that is in Christ Jesus. 25 God presented him as the mercy seat by his blood, through faith, to demonstrate his righteousness, because in his restraint God passed over the sins previously committed. 26 God presented him to demonstrate his righteousness at the present time, so that he would be just and justify the one who has faith in Jesus. -- Romans 3:23-26 (CSB)

6 For while we were still helpless, at the right time, Christ died for the ungodly. 7 For rarely will someone die for a just person — though for a good person perhaps someone might even dare to die. 8

But God proves his own love for us in that while we were still sinners, Christ died for us. 9 How much more then, since we have now been justified by his blood, will we be saved through him from wrath. 10 For if, while we were enemies, we were reconciled to God through the death of his Son, then how much more, having been reconciled, will we be saved by his life. 11 And not only that, but we also boast in God through our Lord Jesus Christ, through whom we have now received this reconciliation. -- Romans 5:6-11 (CSB)

You and I represent ALL who have fallen short, and you and I represent the UNGODLY who needed Christ to die for us!

But also feel this: **We have been made new because of Christ's death, but it doesn't mean we have a license to sin**.

Twice in the first 15 verses of the same chapter, the Apostle Paul says this:

**1 What should we say then? Should we continue in sin so that grace may multiply?
2 Absolutely not! How can we who died to sin still live in it? -- Romans 6:1-2 (CSB)**

15 What then? Should we sin because we are not under the law but under grace? Absolutely not! -- Romans 6:15 (CSB)

It's always crazy to me how we can still choose to dabble in sin willfully when grace frees us from the chains of sin. My response to this grace is not to run back to the disease that led me to death. My response to grace should be running into the arms of the loving father who gave me that grace! It is an abuse of grace to keep sinning willfully!

Dietrich Bonhoeffer calls this cheap grace:

> "Cheap grace is the preaching of forgiveness without requiring repentance, baptism without church discipline, Communion without confession, absolution without personal confession. Cheap grace is grace without discipleship, grace without the cross, grace without Jesus Christ, living and incarnate." [2]

Both Paul and Peter, two men who had crazy former lives, became faithful followers of Jesus and were still not perfect. But they chose not to be exhausted by this quest for perfection when they knew the perfect Savior gave them grace! They would choose repentance over relapse.

Paul became the greatest missionary of all time! Yet, he still struggled with sin in his imperfection:

14 For we know that the law is spiritual, but I am of the flesh, sold as a slave under sin. 15 For I do not understand what I am doing, because I do not practice what I want to do, but I do what I hate. 16 Now if I do what I do not want to do, I agree with the law that it is good. 17 So now I am no longer the one doing it, but it is sin living in me. 18 For I know that nothing good lives in me, that is, in my flesh. For the desire to do what is good is with me, but there is no ability to do it. 19 For I do not do the good that I want to do, but I practice the evil that I do not want to do. 20 Now if I do what I do not want, I am no longer the one that does it, but it is the sin that lives in me. -- Romans 7:14-20 (CSB)

Paul admits the flesh is still at war for his soul!
But then he thanks God for salvation!

24 What a wretched man I am! Who will rescue me from this body of death? 25 Thanks be to God through Jesus Christ our Lord! So then, with my mind I myself am serving the law of God, but with my flesh, the law of sin. -- Romans 7:24-25 (CSB)

Here's what is even crazier about Peter.
Before Peter denied Jesus, Jesus gives him a better calling:

17 Jesus responded, "Blessed are you, Simon son of Jonah, because flesh and blood did not reveal this to you, but my Father in heaven. 18 And I also say to you that <u>you are Peter, and on this rock I will build my church</u>, and the gates of Hades will not overpower it. 19 I will give you the keys of the kingdom of heaven, and whatever you bind on earth will have been bound in heaven, and whatever you loose on earth will have been loosed in heaven." -- Matthew 16:17-19 (CSB)

Ten chapters before Peter denied Jesus, Jesus told Peter that he would build his Church on him! Talk about a better identity! Jesus knew exactly that moment Peter would deny Him, yet still called him The Rock! This means that you may screw up in various chapters of your life, but those chapters are a part of your story, they're not the whole story! You are forgiven and given a new life just like Peter.

I love Brant Hanen's take on this in his book *Unoffendable*:

> "So think about this: When Peter insists that he is even willing to die for Jesus, Jesus tells him, "No, you'll betray Me. You'll deny Me—three times. But don't let your heart be troubled. Believe in me. I'm going to prepare a special place for you—and I'm coming back to get you!"[3]

You may be imperfect, but in Christ you are perfectly saved! And He's coming back to get you!

Peter's label changed from traitor to true testifier!

In Acts 2, Peter preached to thousands of people and led so many to salvation in Jesus.

Peter went from rejecting Jesus to being a part of the revolution![4]

Peter would later be crucified upside down.
In humility, he went from worrying about his greatness to not even considering himself worthy enough to die on the cross the same way Jesus did.

Are you ready to declare you are imperfect and kill the label of perfection?

God's truth is that you are His even when you fail. Everybody fails but everybody can be forgiven.

John says:
16 Indeed, we have all received grace upon grace from his fullness -- John 1:16 (CSB)

Jesus' brother James says:
6 But he gives greater grace -- James 4:6 (CSB)

When you turn to Jesus, grace never ends.
You cannot sin your way out of grace.
No matter how far you run, his grace runs further!

Have you been addicted for years? There's grace
upon grace.
Have you been self-righteous, judging others
severely? There's grace upon grace.

Do you keep failing in relationships and going from
person to person to satisfy a craving? Look, there's
grace upon grace.

Did you leave your parents' house and defy their
authority, and have been living in indulgence,
isolation, and entitlement? There's grace upon grace.

Did you steal from your business? There's grace upon
grace.

Add up everything you have ever done together, and
he still gives greater grace.

There's nothing greater than a Father reminding you
of your status with him.

Lately in my life, I have found more peace than I ever
have by admitting I am not perfect, I have never been
perfect, nor will I ever be perfect till I am called to
heaven. Lately, I have actually listened to Father God

when He tells me I am His beloved child. I have actually started believing that I am loved and that I can love myself! I remind myself that I have been given a former life so that I can now live a faithful one. I remind myself that I am not a failure, I am forgiven.

Remember, you have been made new so that you can walk in that newness!

And even when you fail, remember: **if anyone is in Christ, he is a new creation; the old has passed away, and see, the new has come! -- 2 Corinthians 5:17 (CSB)**

Here are some final steps:

1. *If you want peace, admit you will never be perfect*: Now breathe! You just admitted something freeing. No one places more expectations on you than YOU. This leads to turmoil and chaos. You need someone who is perfect. But first, admit out loud that you will never achieve perfection in this lifetime. You will always need a Savior and it's not you.

2. *Step into God's forgiveness. His forgiveness is greater than your biggest failure:* Confess your failure to God and understand that, through the Cross of Jesus, he destroyed that failure. Embrace the truth that he forgives forever.

3. *Remember that "It is Finished."* Jesus' final words are your new anthem for life. It's not about what you have done, it's about what Jesus has done. The gospel is the good news that Jesus is the perfect substitute for an imperfect person. God sees Jesus in you now. Remember that whenever you feel like you have blown it. Remember that Jesus paid your sin debt, a price you could never pay on your best day. It. Is. Finished!

Reflect:

1. Are you good about moving forward after failing and learning from failure or do you dwell *on* and *in* your failures?

2. Thinking back on the life of Peter, how can you relate to him as a follower of Jesus?

3. What's so good about God's grace? Discuss with someone.

4. Did you know that God knows what you have done, what you are doing, and what you will do, yet still calls you His through His son Jesus? Describe how beautiful that truth is. If you believe that, then it's time to crush the label of perfectionism and to put on Jesus as the ultimate perfect Savior.

CONCLUSION

The book you are holding in your hands almost didn't come out this year. I originally wanted it out in July of 2021. I even posted on Instagram that this book would come out in the summer of 2021. And people were pumped! I was ecstatic to see the response! When I was in middle school all the way through college, I wasn't a great writer. I even called myself stupid and not smart enough. A label and lie I always believed were true. I didn't even like to read at one point in my life, which probably comes as a shock to some! But I know I have always had something to say. I know God called me to communicate and say things for a living.

As I continued to grow in my craft as a preacher and communicator, I also started to get obsessed with reading. In 2017, I read 72 books. In 2018, I read 41 books. In both 2019 and 2020, I read 100 books!

The more books I read, the more I desired to start putting my words on paper. I fell in love with quotes, zingers, phrases, stories, and words in general. So even though I had seminary professors telling me I desperately needed to work on my writing, I discovered that they wanted me to write like them, and not how God has called me to write. Not everyone is called to write dissertations and research books. But someone like me, could take words and phrases, put them in an order that you can understand, so that you can be inspired and impacted.

I finally wrapped up writing this book in April, but I hadn't sent it to my editor. When I was working on a sermon, hustling and hurrying, I spilled an energy drink on my computer. No worries, right? That is if I had saved my book to a drive, had emailed myself, and had it backed up...

It turns out, the computer died, and my book was not backed up nor double backed up and I lost my book. Months and months of hard work and hustle, to get the book on my heart out to people, was deleted forever.

I fell into a week of grief and depression. Frustrated at my clumsy self for having my energy drink next to my computer. Angry at myself for not backing up the book or even sending a copy to myself or the editor. Irritated at my hurried style of work when there was nothing to be in a hurry about. What labels did I give myself? Stupid! Dumb! I almost started to convince myself that this book wasn't supposed to happen, and maybe that was a sign this book would be trash anyways.

I didn't touch this book the whole summer. I didn't even begin to write. The only thing I did was write the sermon series to this book we planned for our Student Ministry. I ended up having a great conversation with my friend Vick Green, who asked if I wanted to be a part of this crew called the Replicate Collective. After months of praying and discovering that this was the level of leadership and community I needed, I accepted and got into a huddle of twelve incredible leaders at various churches across the country. And we were challenged to come up with a professional and personal goal.

I tried to avoid making this book my personal goal. I was that angry and bitter at the fact that I would have to write it from scratch again. I was scared it wouldn't flow as well. But sure enough, I made it my personal goal to hustle harder than ever and write this book so that it could be released in 2021, so I could achieve my year goal and life goal of becoming an author!

And I am very proud to say that this book is in your hands because of the wisdom God gave me, the encouragement the Replicate Collective offered me, the constant love and courage my wife put in me, and the grit I was able to have in the face of straight up doubt and discouragement!

I tell you all of that to say, pursue your dreams. God will wire you and give you the desire to go after what you have been designed for. It will take ignoring the labels others have given you and the labels you have given yourself.

You absolutely can destroy the lies of condemnation and embrace the truth of God's compassion.

You absolutely can destroy the lies of shame and embrace the truth that the savior was shattered so that you can be made whole.

You absolutely can destroy the lies that you are overlooked when the truth is God sees you and believes you were worth dying for.

You absolutely can destroy the lies that your past defines you. The truth is your past can only describe what you have done. But now you have a new identity. You now walk the truth in your faithful life.

You can absolutely destroy the lies that you have to be perfect. Be real. Embrace the truth that only Jesus is perfect and that you be embraced by His grace when you fail.

Don't ever take on a label that God never gave you! It's time to destroy the lies God never gave you and embrace the truths that he has!

ACKNOWLEDGMENTS

I am not smart nor skilled enough to write a book by myself. It takes a team even if it's a team of three!

I want to thank you, Harley Sagrera, for your insight and sharp skill set to make my words and phrases better! Your time and effort in helping me pursue my dreams is so encouraging!

I want to thank you, Haydn Fabre, for your attention to detail and giftedness in creating is unmatched in my opinion! You make content come alive through your images!

I want to thank my jewel, my queen, my wife, Katie Griffon, for believing in me, encouraging me, and being my biggest supporter and fan! I love you!

I also want to thank my Pastor and friend, Sean Walker, for loving me well and for praying for the rewrite of this book. Your prayers have changed the game for me in ways you don't even know!

NOTES

Introduction
1. Powell, Kara Eckmann, and Brad M. Griffin. 3 Big Questions That Change Every Teenager: Making the Most of Your Conversations and Connections. Baker Books, 2021, p. 102
2. Genesis 1:26-27 (CSB):
   [26]Then God said, "Let us make man in our image, according to our likeness. They will rule the fish of the sea, the birds of the sky, the livestock, the whole earth, and the creatures that crawl on the earth." [27]So God created man in his own image; he created him in the image of God; he created them male and female.

Chapter 1 - Daughter
1. Information about Dr. Tony Evan's Kingdom Agenda can be found here: http://tonyevans.org/tony-evans-the-kingdom-agenda/
2. Martin, Charles. What If It's True?: A Storyteller's Journey With Jesus. Thomas Nelson Publishing, 2020. (ibook).
3. Hansen, Brant. The Truth About Us: The Very Good News About How Very Bad We Are. Dreamscape Media, 2020. (ibook).

Chapter 2 - No Longer Condemned
1. "Akubra Girl Dolly's Bullying Suicide Shocks Australia." BBC News, BBC, 10 Jan. 2018, https://www.bbc.com/news/world-australia-42631208. https://www.facebook.com/permalink.php?story_fbid=539369523096711&id=100010710036330

2. NF. "Ten Feet Down." Spotify. https://open.spotify.com/track/68biLwi894rM QPeliSky2t?si=18191a5ed83d47ac

3. Andy Mineo. "Falling?" Spotify. https://open.spotify.com/track/2ERaJ2D0xPDd OmKPyUPxTT?si=afb8ba785ef747ef

4. Hansen, Brant. The Truth About Us: The Very Good News About How Very Bad We Are. Dreamscape Media, 2020. (ibook).

5. Andy Stanley's Twitter statement about kindness: https://twitter.com/andystanley/status/103962 3383091216384

6. Brown, C. Brené. The Gifts of Imperfection: Let Go of Who You Think You're Supposed to Be and Embrace Who You Are, Hazelden Publishing, Center City, MN, 2010, p. 68.

7. "Matt Chandler - Jesus Wants the Rose." YouTube, 7 October 2012, https://youtu.be/bLgIecL1IdY

Chapter 3 - What Does God See?

1. Braveheart. Directed by Mel Gibson, Icon Entertainment International, 1995.

2. Lecrae's quote: Lecrae [@lecrae]. "If you live for people's acceptance, you'll die from their rejection." Twitter, 14 August 2012, https://twitter.com/lecrae/status/235369514517 286912

3. "The Book of Ephesians: J.D. Greear - Ephesians 1:1–14." RightNow Media, https://www.rightnowmedia.org/content/serie s/195647.

Chapter 4 - Our Less Is Him More

1. Elmore, Tim. "How to Turn a Setback into a Comeback." Growing Leaders, 7 May 2020, https://growingleaders.com/blog/how-to-turn-a-setback-into-a-comeback/?mc_cid=4c77b551aa&mc_eid=[2230c31e4f]. Accessed 2021.

2. "Stephen Curry - Success Is Not an Accident (Original)." YouTube, uploaded by Colin Stanton, 3 June 2014, https://www.youtube.com/watch?v=rxsdiusm1NQ.

3. Evans, Tony. The Tony Evans Study Bible: Advancing God's Kingdom Agenda. Holman Bible Publishers, 2019, p. 845.

Chapter 5 - Never Too Far Gone

1. Wright, N. T. Paul: A Biography. Harper One, an Imprint of Harper Collins Publishers, 2018, p. 58.

2. Colossians 3:3 (CSB):
   "For you died, and your life is hidden with Christ in God."

3. Gray, Derwin L., and Beth Moore. The Good Life: What Jesus Teaches about Finding True Happiness. B&H Publishing, 2020. (Kindle)

4. KB, Andy Mineo. "Not Today Satan." Spotify https://open.spotify.com/track/1oKdabnq8pKhjM79yUNN93?si=6c96e4472a6c4647

5. Powell, Kara Eckmann, and Brad M. Griffin. 3 Big Questions That Change Every Teenager: Making the Most of Your Conversations and Connections. Baker Books, 2021.

Chapter 6 - Everyone Fails, Even Christians

1. John 18:10 (CSB):
    "Then Simon Peter, who had a sword, drew it, struck the high priest's servant, and cut off his right ear. (The servant's name was Malchus.)"
2. Bonhoeffer, Dietrich. The Cost of Discipleship For The 21st Century. Reformed Church Publications, 2020, p. 44.
3. Hansen, Brant. Unoffendable: How Just One Change Can Make All of Life Better. W Publishing Group, An Imprint of Thomas Nelson, 2015. (ibook).
4. Acts 2:1-41 (CSB)

Made in the USA
Coppell, TX
16 December 2021